Lightstorm

Lightstorm

An Incredible Journey Of Discovery Into
Consciousness Interdimensional Life & UFO's

R F Allen

BALBOA.
PRESS
A DIVISION OF HAY HOUSE

Hollow Bone Collection
Miami, Florida

Interior Graphics/Art Credit: Robert Allen

Balboa Press books may be ordered through booksellers or by contacting:

Balboa Press
A Division of Hay House
1663 Liberty Drive
Bloomington, IN 47403
www.balboapress.com
1 (877) 407-4847

Print information available on the last page.

ISBN: 978-1-5043-6212-2 (sc)
ISBN: 978-1-5043-6214-6 (hc)
ISBN: 978-1-5043-6213-9 (e)

Library of Congress Control Number: 2016911692

Balboa Press rev. date: 07/18/2016

To
La familia de mi Corazon

Contents

Introduction

I have experienced many other cultures that exist outside of my own. Each culture different from the other. The one thing I have witnessed weaving through every culture is pride. Most of it is to control. 'Do it our way and we will accept you. Do it our way and you will be loved and respected.' Then there are the few that care for you no matter what. They see Compassion in you and you see the Creator in them. They are your true family, no matter what culture they live in. They have risen above their culture.

The most important teaching I can pass on to others is to have an open heart. To Love and receive Love. To teach the mind and the emotions of life to obey the heart. Unconditional Love does not come from emotion, it does not come from the mind, it comes only through the heart. It is invariably linked to Consciousness, the Cosmos, and Infinity.

'Lightstorm' encompasses more than has been previously revealed. Like other books It contains life experiences including heartaches, failures, isolation and rejection. It also contains wisdom learned from those challenges that only helped to magnify the joy, the pure happiness and a greater understanding of Love that came from overcoming those hardships. It contains inter-dimensional photography, messages, and direction for those desiring to elevate their thinking and actions by opening up to their Higher Consciousness.

Many good books have been written about life and its' experiences, however, this book contains something seemingly new . . . yet something that has always existed. This manuscript contains personal accounts, along with pictures from my personal library, of interdimensional life and many of the lifeforms that have visited me over the past few years, relaying messages, showing Unconditional Love. Also showing me my connection, and theirs, with all of humankind.

Over the years I have been approached by many people, throughout my journey, to write about my experiences. I knew that one day I would, but also knew that the timing had to be right. That was many years ago, even before that eye-opening day in 2010, while visiting the Village of Usiacuri in the foothills of the Andes in Colombia, just an hours drive from Barranquilla.

Upon photographing the historic church atop the highest point in the village, I heard that voice inside me say, "Turn and take a picture of the Sun." Without hesitation I did, on that partially cloudy day, not knowing what to expect.

I looked at the picture on the screen of my digital camera and could clearly make out the Sun, clouds, and some other small points of light. I zoomed in on the points of light and saw a geometric design within them.

I looked back up into the sky, at the area where the objects were on the screen, but saw nothing. I thought there must be something to this experience but was unable to scrutinize the photograph further until we returned to the States a few days later.

Upon returning home I downloaded all the digital photographs I took while on our trip. I went directly to the one I took of the Sun and zoomed in on the objects. I was fascinated, excited! I had never seen anything like it. I immediately thought that if it happened in Usiacuri it could happen again right here.

I grabbed my camera, went into the backyard and on that beautiful clear day looked up toward the sun and snapped another picture. That picture is the front cover of this book. My natural eyes saw only the Sun and a clear blue sky but the camera picked up my energy and the energy around the sun that the natural human eye does not detect. I was even more excited than before and began documenting the activity around the sun on a regular basis, and still do to this day.

The time was right to begin writing about my lifetime of experiences and sharing the incredible bond of Love felt in this as well as other dimensions.

The Universe is filled with Light. Light is information. Light is Life in infinite forms and shapes and exists in all frequencies and dimensions. Much of it is benevolent, some is not. I have learned in my journey that we are what we attract. If we choose to live positive lives, contributing to Humankind and the Earth, we attract Light and Lifeforms of the same and higher vibration and grow in understanding of the Cosmos and their interaction with us.

I have photographed many different types and shapes of lifeforms. At first I was startled but have been shown since that Consciousness can enter any lifeform to gain experience. The contact I have made has been with benevolent entities. They have the same desire for Humankind, upon this Earth, as I have, i.e; to reach the full stature of our physical creation understanding the connection with the Cosmos through Consciousness. To learn how to remove the psychological barriers and conditioning we have been programmed to believe over the past 6,000 years. To learn, and show forth Unconditional Love.

This is the Awakening that is taking place throughout the Earth. Many people are asking questions, ones that doubt our need to continue with our existing way of life. That is exactly what is needed. We are finding that the answers are not within the writings, the books, and opinions of others. We are finding that all the answers can be accessed when we go 'within.' We are multi dimensional beings with connections that are Universal not just physical and three dimensional. All the information we seek is available, the key is to seek. Every Soul is intuitive, is psychic, and can amplify that ability through intent. The Cosmos are accessed through intent. We are all connected to the Cosmos. Our intent activates the energy field in and around us and connects with the Cosmos and Light. Light is information and contains the history of the Universes, information that is there for us to receive.

There are no barriers to Light. The only obstacles exist within us do to the conditioning of the world and what we have chosen to believe. It is up to us to deprogram our minds, rid ourselves of this conditioning that has bound humankind for so long. The only barriers present are those we allow. We can eliminate all barriers through intent. The power of creation is within us. We have a direct connection to Source, our Creator.

These bodies we inhabit are vehicles. They are wonderful and perfect creations that allow Consciousness to enter and experience life in this three dimensional world. To experience all emotion, that is only available to us, Consciousness, through this means. When this process of learning is complete, Consciousness simply ascends to a higher dimension with the body, or if not complete, leaves it and enters into another phase of existence to prepare for another body, or vehicle, since it had not fully progressed to the level of Ascension.

You are the key to your Awakening. It will not come from an outside source. Help is available at all levels and throughout all dimensions but the intent to Awaken comes from within you. The intent of 'Lightstorm' is to assist in that Awakening.

Chapter 1

Conduit to Higher Consciousness

The scientific world has proven what many people throughout history have known, the existence of other dimensions, and are researching how to access them. Scientists are acknowledging that life can exist in many different forms, environments, frequencies, and dimensions. They do not readily admit the existence of Consciousness, which is separate from the body.

The Ancients were able to understand, even see and interact with some of these lifeforms and environments. Scientists are attempting to prove their findings through technology because society has severed the Spirit connection through conditioning and deception. Some of our ancestors, Ancients, understood the Spirit connection and handed down that knowledge of Spirit and Consciousness to posterity. They knew what it meant to be a conduit between this plane of existence and higher frequencies and dimensions. They did not know the word 'conduit.' They referred to it as becoming like a 'hollow bone,' to access and channel Higher Consciousness to themselves and teach others to do likewise.

Key individuals, sometimes called Witch Doctors, Medicine Men or Shaman, knew how to attain an altered state of Consciousness. Many through ingesting certain plants, barks and roots in special ceremonies, as well as rhythmic sounds and chants. These altered states permitted the Shaman to enter different vibrations within this dimension. Then there were those that could travel there simply by altering their brain frequency and heart vibration without outside assistance.

We live in a three dimensional world. The fourth dimension includes what religion teaches as the Spirt World, a place where the Spirit goes after death to rest, or suffer, depending on our actions during mortality.

The forth dimension is much more than that and can be accessed while still in mortality. Fear can open the door to negative energy in that dimension, while Love can attract positive energy from the same place.

The fifth dimension is accessed through an open heart. As a person seeks to know truth, they eventually come to a knowledge of Universal Consciousness. At that moment the heart opens fully to receive understanding regarding the inquiry. All higher knowledge can be accessed this way. The door has been opened to the individual and all access is granted as the knowledge and power of the human heart melds with Universal Consciousness. At this point you have entered into the true 'natural state' of the heart. The true understanding of Unconditional Love is known and is then a natural reflex and is programmed into subconscious.

There are many dimensions, perhaps infinite. Within each dimension are frequencies. A good analogy of this is the existence of radio waves. We know they exist in our dimension because we have radios and televisions to tune-in to them, but first the radio waves had to be discovered. This happened through the implanting of ideas leading to inventions through technology from creator gods within this third dimension, not visible to us because they are hidden in different frequencies. Some ideas and inventions have come through higher Consciousness. Multiple frequencies exist within each dimension and contain life and lifeforms that are beginning to re-reveal themselves. Science will find a way to move within the third dimension through technology because there are those who will not acknowledge that other dimensions can be accessed by anything other than three dimensional technology. The knowledge to access higher frequencies and dimensions is within the grasp of each human being as they invite higher vibrations into their heart. Technology is the 'bull in the china cupboard.' It is the only way available to the unawakened individual.

The gods of history are not thousands of years more advanced than us, they are only a 'frequency modulation' more advanced, and they are not gods! They are not even of a higher dimension. They are inhabitants of the same dimension as us at this point-in-time. The main differences between us is that they do not have physical bodies but they do have a somewhat higher technology than we, at our frequency, and they have known how to 'tune-in' to us. They have used their knowledge of technology to make us 'tune-out' to their existence. Some entities with these capabilities have used them to deceive and control because of our ignorance and we have believed them throughout history. They have been very adept at using 'interactive holograms' to deceive mankind into believing the apparitions and visions seen by religious leaders and religious followers, which had a supposedly divine source. In-fact, the source of these 'visions' was intradimensional, from within our own dimension. Their holographic projectors are concealed within a frequency that we at present can't access.

The worship and fear of a jealous God is what religion has been based on from the beginning. There is nothing higher than Love, nor greater. Worshipping and fearing God and following His/Her commandments are not, nor have ever been, directives from Source. These are nothing more than rules designed and put into effect to control the masses and the direction of this world. The whole idea from the beginning of this cycle of civilization, the past 6,000 years, was to get mankind to fear and worship creator gods, who exist within our own dimension only at a different frequency.

Supreme Creator, Source, radiates Love. Worship and fear are left to those who choose to exercise control over mankind because they have the free agency to do so and we have the free agency to accept it or not. The key has been their ability to deceive us through their understanding of technology and frequency through the use of interactive holograms manipulating us to believe they were in charge and that there was no higher source. They blocked higher information from our awareness and we, as humankind have followed them like sheep. In themselves, they cannot damage or destroy the Earth, however, they have been allowed to manipulate mankind to damage and destroy to inject fear and control.

We haven't dared question them, until now, due to the fear they had conditioned us to believe in. The teachings of a jealous, vengeful yet loving God permeates all of religion, even today. These creator gods have nourished themselves by the energy produced through mankind's fear and intimidation of them.

Worldly Knowledge

We have been conditioned to believe that Universities are institutions of higher learning. Not so! Higher learning is achieved only through accessing Universal Consciousness where we are in contact with our higher self. All knowledge available to those who enter in.

Universities access world knowledge and claim it is higher learning. It involves nothing more than promoting the ways of the world and of corrupt man and the creator gods. This is brainwashing and conditioning of the mind and heart. Many professionals at that level pride themselves in teaching students to be free thinkers, as long as it fits into their mold or concept of what they think the world should be.

The Hippie movement of the 1960s' introduced some creative thinking to 'rock the boat' of present thinking at that time. Some of their beliefs were inspired through Higher Consciousness and again, just like at the time of the cultural revolution 1900 years prior, clever leaders both ecclesiastical and political began to manipulate the hippie way of thinking. Clever leaders began to tell the 'flower children' that if they wanted to change the 'system' they had to first become part of the 'system,' to change it from within. The very same is happening with the Tea Party. They are voted in to eventually be swept up into the same 'system' that has caused the world so much misery, disappointment, and death through justifiable actions in order to preserve and protect our so called 'sacred way of life'!

The Source

The seeker of truth understands, eventually, that the student can only access truth through entering into Universal Consciousness which is the fountain of all Truth and knowledge. The individual must enter in on their own, enhance their intuitiveness, increasing their ability to listen, realizing that life exists in all times, dimensions, and Universes. As this is realized the individual rises above this world, feels the Spirit connection with the Earth and all of Creation. The individual then becomes an enemy of the world but is then a friend and sustainer of the Earth and its mission.

I am giving you a glimpse into the Heart of God (Source). Source is not complicated. Source does not issue doctrines nor commandments. We are all connected to one another. We are all connected to Source. Source is in us, literally.

Earth has a Soul too. It exercises its own free agency. We have been given free agency also. It was intended that humankind would become one with the Earth, however, within a very short time, during this cycle of civilization, some members of humankind developed ways, working through intradimensional gods, to establish a 'pay as you go' system of control, introducing fear, greed, and power over others.

The energy produced by these negative teachings was food for the gods. Their human counterparts claimed inspirations, revelations, and visions from them, insisting that humankind must be obedient and submissive to them or suffer death (the inquisition), and eternal damnation.

The way of the Creator is that all life be blessed by the Earth freely, and give back to the Earth freely, and to one another. Were there a way for the powers that be to tax the air we breathe and the rain that nourishes the Earth, it would have been done long ago. We exist in the lowest vibration of Three Dimensional existence. It is beyond the understanding of other extraterrestrial civilizations, that know of our world, how we have to pay our way to exist on a sphere that was created for us as a gift to inhabit freely, out of Love. Life upon this planet was meant to be free, to be shared, experienced and enhanced through the pure energy that is Unconditional Love. To help one another in all aspects of our created environment, not to see how much we could gain by taxing other peoples efforts and property to enhance another's physical status while sacrificing the wants and needs of those now seemingly inferior.

Earth A Free-Will Planet

Earth is a free-will planet and intradimensional beings have taken advantage of it, introducing power and control through fear. As they did they also commanded honor and worship due to their more advanced knowledge of technology, frequency, and the Universe, intimidating man into believing they would suffer the consequences of sin and rebellion, even to the destruction of Earth itself. Knowing that we had not developed to the same level, and with strategic visits to this

Earth frequency, they counted on the fact that they could control us. Keeping Humankind under control through fear was the key.

Though the hands of those that deceived have been tied and they cannot introduce their ideas anymore, they have been quite thorough through power hungry humans who still use these techniques, many not even knowing they were originally from intradimensionals. The truth is that Humankind has had its attention diverted and been more concerned with their credit score than they have been in accessing Universal Consciousness. There again, fear over Love.

Earth Ascending

The earth is moving into a higher level of Consciousness and is recompensing man for its misuse! As the Earth moves into a higher level, those of humankind who are aware of this, and desire to, are also moving into it. They are connected to the Earth, Universal Consciousness, and Source.

The manipulation of evil has been perfected through religions, governments, and corporations.

Life exists throughout the universes and dimensions. Humans have the ability to create at a subordinate level. Creation at lower vibrations, within the Third Dimension, can and has been realized on this earth like no other. Interference of intradimensional travelers, with an understanding of higher three dimensional technology, have been regular visitors throughout our history. These 'travelers' have been honored and worshipped as gods down through the eons of time. They are the same intruder gods of Hinduism as in the 'one true God' of Monotheism. They are all impostors and, at this time, have had their freedom of movement and interference blocked concerning this Earth, as Higher Consciousness and higher creations are here to assist. Creation by the highest source has always been done through Love. Love is the power to create at the highest level. The Earth is ascending rapidly. This world will be left behind to continue floundering in its' own disbelief, continuing to feed the Intradimensional deity through their misplaced energy.

History Repeating Itself

There has been sufficient time to change this direction without intervention. Religion refers to a divine deliverance in 'the last days', even a 'rapture' or being caught up into the clouds to be saved while the earth is cleansed by fire.

As in the times of Moses, there will be a deliverance. That deliverance 3500 years ago (not 3200 years according to archaeologists), was not a 'divine' deliverance but an interdimensional one. The people cried out to 'their God' to be saved from the political and religious control they had been enduring in Egypt. Their prayers were answered in a way they could not comprehend as anything less than miraculous. Moses understood the interdimensional as well as the intradimensional connection. It was his destiny during that lifetime. The deliverance was not a one sided event. There was a need created. Moses fled the Egyptian culture to a wilderness where he could be contacted, taught, and sent back to help free the people.

Although Moses understood the interdimensional/intradimensional connection he could not teach the entirety of the Children of Israel since they were so steeped in the superstition of their ancestors as well as the powerful Egyptian form of worship and adoration of the Pharaohs that had been the cause of their enslavement for several generations. Religion played a powerful role in the ancient world as it has until today.

Moses had to have lived a very solitary life in that he understood the powers behind the religions at the time but could say very little. He was regarded as God to many of those delivered and there was such ignorance in the majority of the 13 Tribes at the time, that he had to set up a system to govern them.

The Ten Commandments were introduced to the body of Israel and administered to the Israelites by certain individuals, leaders that were chosen by Moses. They were more teachable. Moses had been taught by the 'The Ancients' while in the wilderness; higher guides and messengers during the years he was preparing to return to Egypt to deliver the people.

He had a close relationship with his brother Aaron upon his return to Egypt before the Exodus. He taught Aaron about the interdimensional/intradimensional connection as he was destined to assist in the deliverance of the Israelites. He, according to the Torah, was a mouthpiece for Moses and was involved in the 'miracles' that were precursors to the freeing of the enslaved by the Pharaoh. Aaron was aware of the interdimensional/intradimensional connection and had experiences of his own to help prepare him and the other men of the Tribe of Levi in being 'called' as priests to administer the sacred, or spiritual ceremonies to the remaining 12 tribes of Israel.

The same process is underway today. It is repeating itself. Many have cried out for assistance, even non-religious people. What I have observed is that many people in the western world don't even realize they are in bondage. This time it is to the powers that are in charge of the free world. Our world is not free. We are conditioned from birth to believe we are free. We are acclimated in our culture to accept things as they are and that they cannot be changed so the culture is accustomed to governments 'fixing' the problem by putting a band-aid over the incurable cancer and convincing the masses that everything is, or will be okay. It is not okay! The cancer remains and is only getting worse!

Today there are many more who understand the universal order of things. More than at the time of Moses. That we are part of a greater community. A community motivated by Love, by connection, even interdimensional connection, knowing that we are all one, one with Source.

A 'deliverance' is under way. To many it will seem miraculous. To others it is not miraculous because they understand their connection to Source. It is being done through Love. The Love that our interdimensional family has for us, and we for each other, and our desire to live life with joy, without fear. However, our interdimensional family is not forcing this deliverance. They are here by invitation. Earth itself is ascending in its Consciousness. We can be one with it. We can and will ascend together as we choose. Those who do not wish to ascend at this time are not lost nor condemned as religion would have them believe. They will ascend at their own pace. No one is forced to ascend. All life is connected to Source whether we ascend now or through another lifetime.

Those who appear to be the greatest and most powerful in the world today will soon become the 'enchained,' bound by their own greed, control, and appetite for power, where those preparing to ascend are concerned. Religion is being exposed for what it has done to the world. It is in the process of devouring itself. Truth is invading religion. People are awakening. This must happen. It can be no other way and with the demise of religion will come the dissolving of borders, physical and spiritual, and all types of corrupt political and corporate control in regards to those ascending. Crime will diminish because fear will have lost its foothold in that arena. Fear will be understood and its systematic introduction into culture and society over the millennia. The intradimensional source of fear is also, even now, being eliminated and can be seen by those who choose to see. All this is in process at a higher vibration and those who choose to ascend will be partakers of this new world.

This is the new world unfolding, but what about those who are not ready or wanting to ascend at this time? What happens to them?

Author Dolores Cannon describes it in this way;

> "This earth is preparing to separate into two earths. One earth remaining in this present dimension while the other moves into the Fifth Dimension. Those prepared to ascend will do so with the new earth while those not prepared or not wanting to leave the Third Dimension will remain."

There will be catastrophic events that will affect the remaining Three Dimensional plane of existence. There will be survivors, however, they may be starting over with society, having to begin a new cycle of civilization.

Cycles of civilization have taken place in the past. A new cycle is about to begin.

As we access Higher Consciousness we will literally rise above this world. We will not experience the so called Apocalypse but we may be allowed to view it from our new Earth.

Chapter 2

The Strawberry Patch

Pure truth has never come to me from outside sources yet the world and religion teaches precisely this, that all truth can only come to mankind through inspired educators and men of God. Many of the most devastating teachings have come from the pulpit. It has been a fountain of deception throughout the ages. Religion has conditioned humankind to believe that it is the only source of truth, and that it must be embraced at all cost, while sacrificing individual freedoms and rights. To promote it at all cost, financial and spiritual, or suffer an eternity in hell.

Many of the greatest teachings I have received in my life came through my father. They began in the strawberry patch, in the garden he prepared himself, for family sustenance, and to take advantage, as he found time, to spend one on one with me. Those teachings were very motivating, but only I could discover whether they were from a higher Source and truthful. As a young boy he told me that the most important thing I could do in life was to 'seek God with all my heart.' Those words resonated in me like a golden bell. They were words well placed in my pathway, to set me on my destined course. That powerful message uttered by my father came from his lips but they were already in my heart. His words awakened me because I recognized them in me.

This book, the photographs, and messages that accompany them, are meant to help awaken you, or to further awaken you to your destiny, to encourage you to find your own path. To show where truth is found and can be accessed through your own intent.

I began meditating, contemplating those powerful words of my father. I didn't even know what meditation meant then, but realized at a later age that I had always been meditating. Religion taught me how to pray, to form the words, not how to really connect with my Source. It taught me that I was required to ask 'Heavenly Father in the name of Jesus Christ' in order to receive answers to my requests and if I didn't receive an answer it simply was not meant to be or I was asking in the wrong way. Religions' methodical way of introducing guilt into the seeking individual when not getting the desired answer, or any answer.

Religion wanted me to be the one to blame for not doing it correctly. I wasn't the only one experiencing the guilt, all my family and other Mormon friends seemed to be struggling with the same feeling of falling short of perfection. I found throughout the following years, as I learned about other churches, that most Christians felt the same. All churches taught that the Bishop, Pastor, Reverend, Priest or whatever titled leader stood at the pulpit, had the authority to tell his members how to live their life so the church could prosper financially and the obedient membership could find grace through that religion hoping they would be admitted into heaven at the appropriate time, either at death or at the Second Coming of their Savior.

Even at a young age I felt confusion in the teachings of that religion. My father taught me I was a son of God. My intent was to access God directly. Why did I have to do it through Jesus? I didn't have anything against him, I simply felt I could talk to God directly, after all, He was my Father, right?

The times I spent in the family garden, beginning when I was eight, would find me reflecting on my fathers words because that is where I was helping him when he told me what was most important in life. I have thought countless times how much better this world would be if every father worked with his young son in the garden and shared those powerful words that could have only come from the heart.

As I communicated with Source, I, at times, would be taken up in Spirit to a place I could not describe in words. A place of peace, a place of pure joy, of happiness where fear did not exist. I was aware of my body, that it was in a complete physical state, yet my Consciousness was at a higher dimension, aware of, and in the place I longed to be. In my body I was still picking strawberries in the garden. I kept these experiences to myself aside from telling my father of them.

Though I was taken up to that place from time to time I was not given all the answers to the Universe. I sensed I was on a life long journey and was given a Divine understanding that through this journey would come all the answers, and much Wisdom.

My family religion did not make this possible, only my fathers words and my desire to find and communicate with that Source.

I also realized at a young age that it was up to me to put forth the effort to access what I came to know as Universal Consciousness. This did not take place because of words spoken from a pulpit. It happened while I was picking strawberries with my father those early mornings in our family garden. A quiet time when a loving father would reach out to his son and give him a simple truth that would set him on his chosen path for life.

As each person seeks their own answers, with no preconceived notions of how it should be, the Source of all Knowledge opens its embrace and teaches through Spirit, Light, and Energy, in other words, Love. Receiving Truth (Source) becomes a natural event.

The religion of my youth taught that the "Glory of God is Intelligence, or in other words Light and Truth." My connection with Source showed me that the "Glory of God" is 'Creation,' and that it is done simply through Love. We are all Loves creation.

I also came to know that God is not a 'resurrected being.' An exalted man who lived on another Earth where he attained godhood through obedience to religious practices and dogma as taught by my family religion. I will describe the flow of events and how they were choreographed and how the same process was used throughout the history of religion, in another chapter.

The most important thing each person can do is to go within. Ignoring the teachings and conditioning of the world. We are divine creations. We have Source within. That understanding gives us power over the world, over the circumstances of life that we have been conditioned to accept. We can still live within the existing world while changing it at the same time.

Find your direction within. Become more intuitive. Listen to your Source. Do not accept the world as it is. Question everything! When presented with instructions or advise from others, go within to the Source to confirm or reject.

As you develop your intuition you can receive immediate answers to your queries. The speed of thought is faster than the speed of light. You will witness yourself changing, metamorphicizing. This, then, is the foundation of Wisdom. As your Knowledge of the Universe increases so does your desire to help others. You come to the realization that the only requirement is 'to do unto others as you would have them do unto you.' In that simple teaching rests Eternity, Universal Consciousness, Love of self and all of Creation.

Become one, again, with Source, as you were at birth and before.

Universal Consciousness in based on Love, and is Love. Religion is based in fear.

Throughout history all wars can be traced back to religion as the root cause.

Religion is where people freely placed, or were forced and intimidated to place, blind faith. Where power has been given to ecclesiastical leaders to be in charge of their spiritual and physical well being. In doing so they gave them authority to manipulate their past, present, and future through doctrines and commandments of that jealous god. A person can be non-religious, and even atheist, and give the same control over to a political party or movement. It does not always mean a church. It can be, and quite often is, a private organization, a corporation, a culture, the stock market, anything that is allowed to exercise control over ones life, quite often at the invitation of the individual, sometimes through force, as seen in fascist governments and dictatorships. Power and Control are the motivating factors nurtured through fear. Humanity has been persuaded by the need to be lead by more inspired leaders, that people are like sheep needing direction.

An excellent example of religions domination is through that of the Universal Church. It came into being as the result of a political movement not a spiritual one. There were Christian teachings virtually outlawed by the Council of Constantine because they interfered with the possibility of loss of control by the church and government.

Hidden Teachings

The roots of Christianity included the teachings of reincarnation. It taught that the Soul would eventually attain perfection that it was not able to in previous incarnations. The Bible itself spoke of this. When Jesus was asked by his disciples to tell them more about John, who was the Baptist, he said they would not believe him. They insisted they would, so he told them, "This is Elijah who was to come." Then the disciples understood that John and Elijah (Elias) were one, and the same.

The resurrection and Judgement Day teachings were not introduced until the fourth century. Corresponding precisely with the outlawing of the teaching of reincarnation. Obviously the church believed that teaching reincarnation would weaken it as it would offer an alternative to a one life, one judgement doctrine. Later on, it was declared heresy and many of those who continued to believe were put to death. The Judgement Day teaching was necessary to intimidate followers into obedience to religion, and thus the State, likewise, the teaching of resurrection. All part of the well orchestrated manipulation of the new Christian world.

Ascension was one of the open teachings until that time. The teaching of Ascension has always existed, but like other truths masked by greed for power, it has seemingly been hidden from the world. Finally, after nearly two millennia, many are freeing themselves from the deception that has flooded the world in both Eastern and Western society.

How Does This Affect Me?

What can you do? If you are reading this book you are already on your own appointed path. Look for truth. Confirm with your Higher Self. Follow your heart. Listen to that voice within. Become more intuitive. Do unto others. In doing these things you open up your heart to direction from Source. You understand your connection to Source and truly show Unconditional Love. The world, as it has been, will become unrecognizable being brought into the glory that the Creator intended, and it will have come about due to our exercising free agency, by choosing to live by higher principles and eternal truths that have always existed but have been mostly hidden until now.

Divine Light showered down on me in that strawberry patch, and with it I would be able to experience much joy, but also many hardships during my life. Many experiences I would keep to myself until I was in a position to share them with others through my teachings, lectures, and writings. All this began in the family garden when I was a boy.

Chapter 3

Dedication To A Cause

My father had been raised by his widowed mother who was a Mormon and, although not active in the religion, made sure that all her children were baptized at the age of eight and all the male children were ordained to the priesthood as early as twelve years of age.

My Grandfather died just a few days prior to my fathers fourth birthday. My grandmother never remarried. She was not well educated and spent many years doing laundry and scrubbing floors to earn money to feed her seven children. She died of old age at fifty-three. The older children worked at whatever they could to help my Grandmother feed and clothe their brothers and sisters. They would walk the tracks, after a train went through town, looking for chunks of coal that had fallen off the cars and sell them in town for a few cents.

At eight years of age my father was sent to live with an aunt and uncle on their ranch near Pinedale, Wyoming, several hours north of Rock Springs where he was born. Although baptized, he knew nothing about the religion. His religion became the outdoors . . . nature. From eight years of age until he left Pinedale with his new bride at his side thirteen years later, he lived and breathed the wilderness of the Wind River Mountains.

He became a surveyor and worked on the crews building the 'Lincoln Highway' across Wyoming. He and my mother would migrate to Spokane, Washington in 1943 to work for Henry Kaiser who was building an aluminum rolling mill. All part of the stimulus brought on by World War II.

He would tell me of those years going for a beer after work with his buddy's and having contests flipping cockroaches across the bar.

Hell, I Am One!

Sometime in 1945 my parents received a knock on their door. It was Sunday. My father answered. There stood two men dressed in suits introducing themselves as missionaries. They asked Dad if he had ever heard of the Mormons.

Dad responded, "Hell, I am one!"

He invited them in and there began the religious indoctrination of an entire generation setting my father on his self-appointed course to bring all of his brothers and sisters and their spouses into church membership and activity.

My mother didn't want to join him in the church. She had been brought up in a non-religious home, in-fact one that had a strong dislike for the Mormon faith. Both her parents had died a few years earlier so she didn't have to face pressure and ridicule from them as her spouse became dedicated to spreading his new faith.

One Sunday as he returned home from his church services she confronted him.

"Why are you so dedicated to this? You're so different now," she said.

His simple reply was, "Would you rather have me the way I was or the way I am now?"

She couldn't argue with him. He had become structured in his direction in life. He loved his family so much. He studied every evening and spent weekends doing missionary work with the same men that had knocked on the door a few months earlier. He wanted to help people. He loved the change religion had made in his life and wanted to share it with everyone. His dedication convinced my mother and she was baptized a few weeks later.

With two little children in tow they adapted fully to Mormon doctrine. After my mother had been a worthy member for one year both she and my father would obtain 'temple recommends', a proof of worthiness, and be 'sealed' in the Salt Lake City temple in October 1946.

My mother had complications in child birth and was told by the doctor that she would be unable to bare more children. On July 4, 1947, almost nine months to the day after their 'sealing' in the temple, I was born. My father would tell me when I was older that I was their covenant child, a miracle from God because of their dedication to Him and the church. My mother would go on to give birth to four more daughters.

From the time I was a child taking my first steps I was told about the 'true church' and how God spoke to a young man of fourteen. How he would receive visitations from 'heavenly messengers' over the next ten years and how the 'keys of the restoration' would be brought to him so he could restore the 'true church' that Jesus had established but was taken away from the earth with the death of His Apostles.

Joseph Smith would receive visitations from Adam, Enoch, Noah, Abraham, Moses, Elijah, and John the Baptist along with Jesus Christ and other heavenly messengers. He would receive many visitations from Moroni, an ancient American prophet, who would present him with golden plates that would reveal the stories now contained in the Book of Mormon. Joseph would translate the 'reformed Egyptian' hieroglyphs recorded on the gold plates by Moroni and his father Mormon some fourteen hundred years earlier. The plates were hidden away in a stone box prepared by Moroni around 421 a.d. in what is now upstate New York near Palmyra in a hill called Cumorah.

Joseph declared the translation was correct because he used an instrument, provided by Moroni, called a Urim and Thummim. It was a gold breastplate with two arms extending from it and on the end of the two arms were 'seer stones', celestial rocks, touched by God Himself. They were semitransparent. As he looked through the stones toward the gold plates the ancient recorded language would appear to him in his modern day English. A scribe was on the other side of a curtain that separated the two men. He recorded the words Joseph spoke but was not allowed to see the gold plates.

Mormonism is founded upon the Book of Mormon. Joseph Smith taught his congregations until his death in 1844 that the Book of Mormon was the cornerstone of the Church of Jesus Christ of Latter-day Saints. The most accurate of all his declarations.

He declared the Book of Mormon a second witness of Jesus Christ. That He lived, was crucified and resurrected three days later then ascended to heaven. After that, He appeared as a resurrected being to many of the inhabitants of the Americas. He taught them and walked among them then ascended again into heaven.

If there was no resurrection there is no foundation, not only for Mormonism but for all of Christianity.

The thought of there never having been a resurrection is something active Christians and Mormons are unable to grasp. It is simply unthinkable, yet recorded history does not defend the Jesus story and a resurrection as described in the New Testament.

I wondered what the truth was?

I Was Just An Average Kid

I have never considered myself better than anybody else. In fact, there were many times I felt inferior to others. I was an average student. I liked learning but always felt that many of the subjects were not well thought out and were taught as fact not theory, even at my young age. I was slow to catch on to new subjects, especially Math. I was a slow reader until I was placed in a summer reading program in the 4th grade. I finally caught on and caught up to my peers.

At fourteen, when my friends were entering High School, I didn't attend. Instead, I worked as a labor missionary under my father's direction, on a large church structure he was in charge of building in Montevideo, Uruguay. There were other labor missionaries too, most of them indigenous, from the interior of the country. They spoke no English so I was thrown into the culture and able to learn Spanish quickly.

After six months my father was asked to assume the responsibility of managing projects throughout the Spanish speaking countries of South America and I entered The British School where my two oldest sisters were attending. It was a private institution and we were required to wear uniforms.

I learned a lot about the British system of education. The Prefecture system of governing, the Old Boy's program, the love of the English for Shakespeare, and their love of the on-campus Pub, where some professors spent more time than in the classroom. I began to grasp geometry and solid geometry. My English Literature professor taught Shakespeare with a passion and instilled in me a love for the master. He was also my Geography professor. He taught it with less passion but with equal dedication and I gained a healthy respect for him and a tremendous love for geography. The same was to be said for my Physics and Chemistry professor. She was an American teaching in a British school but taught with equal passion.

I guess I was like most other American students. I excelled in classes I liked and was average in those I didn't. To my surprise I passed the Cambridge Entrance Exam required of every fifteen year old within the British system.

I was only fifteen but already six feet tall and loved sports like most teenagers. I couldn't play football with my friends back in the States so I did the best I could. I learned to love Rugby and still do today.

Though only fifteen, The Old Boys Rugby team, nineteen years and older, asked me to join them on their tour of Argentina and Chile. I declined, feeling uncomfortable about it since their way of life was more open in a worldly sense than my religious upbringing taught me to be.

A few years later one of the Old Boys teams from the Christian Brothers School, just down the road from my school, would find themselves crash landing in the Andes on their way to a game in Chile, and survived for weeks in the sub freezing temperature before being rescued. They were the same boys I played against on the younger team a few years before.

I returned to America at sixteen for more schooling while the rest of my family remained in Uruguay. I felt like an outsider since I was out of my culture. Some times I wondered what my culture was, having come to the little town of Lyman, Wyoming from Montevideo, Uruguay. While I was in High School I excelled only in Music, Photography, and Sports and kept my grades just high enough in the other classes to allow me to play in the school sports programs.

Rebels Bombing The City

Meanwhile, my parents transferred to Guatemala while I completed my senior year at Lyman. In May 1965, upon graduating, I flew down to Guatemala City to spend the summer with them and return to the States in August when my father would complete his contract.

While there, I would witness the bombing of the city by guerrillas coming in out of their jungle hiding places to destroy petroleum storage tanks, an Olympic swimming arena, and homes of politically connected individuals.

One of my sisters and I were watching the bombs explode in the distance at the oil refinery and swimming complex. We were a bit nervous but felt we were in a protected part of the city. As we were discussing the events taking place, 300 feet across the Avenida, a bomb exploded at the residence of one of the politicians earmarked for death by the rebels. The explosion ripped off the wrought iron gates and the front of the house. We had been standing on the fourth floor balcony of our apartment building. The concussion from the blast threw us back against the sliding glass doors. We remained outside to see the police arrive and determine the damage and identify if there was loss of life. Thankfully there wasn't. These attacks against the government would go on for years before there would be any reconciliation. We always felt a level of divine protection even though we were nervous.

Preparing For Her!

We drove back to the States at the end of August that year. Mom would fly back with my two youngest sisters while Dad and I took turns driving the family car back from Guatemala, through Mexico to Laredo, Texas and on to Utah with my three oldest sisters. It was a journey I still remember to this day. The beauty of Mexico should be seen by all. In the jungle just South of Tapachula, at dusk, millions of frogs jumped upon the paved, elevated highway to bask in the remaining heat of the day. The pavement was covered completely. I can still hear the crunching of the little creatures under our tires as we drove along for several miles just as the sun was setting.

The trip took four days and we were glad to be back in the States. My parents would rent a home in Salt Lake City, on the Avenues at the North end overlooking the city. The home was older but in good repair. My parents needed to rest for a few months while deciding their next move. My brother lived a few blocks away with his wife. I stayed with my parents and five sisters.

Our rented home had only three bedrooms so I slept on the screened-in back porch until cold weather set in. By the middle of October I had transferred my mattress to an unfinished side room on the second floor. It was more for attic storage though it had a full size door entryway. I liked the little cubby hole. My mattress fit perfectly. If I wanted to read I would use a flashlight or open the door and use the hall light.

A Deep Sleep

One night I fell deeply into sleep. I awakened and found myself in another attic type room. Unlike mine, it was finished. There was wallpaper on the plastered walls. It had a pitched ceiling and at the gable end a window that allowed a view of green fields as far as I could see on the bright sunlit day. Someone was there with me. I turned and, without hesitation, embraced her. I didn't know her name at the time but would know many years later. The name didn't matter, we knew each other! We kissed, passionately, and made love on the bed, the only piece of furniture in the room. It was unlike anything I had ever experienced in my life. I wasn't a young, brainwashed Mormon boy at that moment. I knew we were connected. The passion was real. The Love was real. The climax was more than sensational! I was sexually pure by church standards and I was still pure after making love to her. Religion did not enter into the experience. Only Love enveloped in passion.

My parents had taught me that a relationship with the right person would bring great joy and peace in my life, but they never said anything about the passion I felt woven into the Love I was experiencing at that moment. I knew I was in a special place in time and it was driven home in a harsh way as I opened my eyes and saw again the walls and roof of my little attic bedroom. She was gone! The pure joy I had felt just moments before was replaced with incredible anguish. I wept. The connection was severed and I felt I was not going to find her again, but at least I had the memory and the vision that was her face and the moments we spent in that attic bedroom.

The next morning I had to tell someone about the experience. I confided in one of my sisters.

I told her about much of what had happened to me in my journey during the night and began to describe her features. She had dark piercing eyes, a beautiful complexion, and dark flowing hair. Then I went on to tell her that she looked similar to a friend of ours from Uruguay. I knew it was only a comparison. There was no connection other than that.

I believe that consciously and subconsciously, from then on, I was looking for her.

Jumping Through Hoops

After that emotional, interdimensional event I did go on to College. I also began cramming for my mission. An obligation in my family. It was not what I wanted to do. I was eighteen and was expected to go out and preach to people about Mormonism and do my best to convert them as soon as I reached my nineteenth birthday. A mission of twenty-seven months at that age seemed like an eternity.

I went, I served, and even excelled. I was the perfect picture of a Mormon missionary. It was the most difficult thing I had ever done up to that point in my life. Before I left for my mission I did have the strength to tell my parents I was doing it because of my Love for, and obedience to them, not to the church.

The thing I did learn while in the mission field was my ability to effect change for the better in peoples lives. I found that my words had power and people believed them. It became my passion, but, to effect change in peoples lives meant to do it with Unconditional Love not to manipulate them to believe the way I was taught. I didn't even believe all that I was required to teach others about Mormonism on my mission. I found myself watching very carefully how I spoke and taught others interested in hearing what I had to say. I felt a tremendous responsibility to speak from the heart even if it didn't always exalt the church.

After completing the twenty-seven month assignment I returned to College and challenged as many courses as I dared, so I wouldn't have to stay there any longer than necessary. I cashed in on my language background and advanced quickly but left college before graduating to pursue a life the University could not teach me in their classrooms.

I would begin my journey of discovery. A journey that would lead me to many countries and cultures. Many truths and many misconceptions of truth.

Chapter 4

Stepping Out On Our Own

I left University life before graduating, having been recruited by an international banking firm. I attended special courses in their overseas banking program excited at the opportunities it could provide me worldwide.

I had always been 'listening' to my heart and had received a strong feeling that I should, and would travel, one day, to Samoa in the South Pacific to work and assist the people of the Islands. That feeling in my heart took on a significant part of my thoughts of the future. I also felt that the appropriate doors would open to direct me to the realization of that event.

Several months later my parents settled in San Diego, California where I was living. With my fathers reputation in custom building, and his international construction experience, he was talked out of retirement to build a beautiful home in El Cajon for an insistent friend. Word spread fast and other opportunities presented themselves. He approached me with the idea of training me to take over his company. After some personal debating, and evaluating of the opportunity, I accepted his offer and we began working together again after eight years. This time there would be a more personal reason and direction in his recruiting me. Being unaware myself, he had seen me wavering in my dedication to the church and felt he could make a difference in influencing me to remain active.

My brother was working for a surveying firm in Kansas City, Mo. and, knowing that we had begun construction on two custom construction projects in California, invited us to join forces with him by transferring our business to Missouri upon completion of the contracts. The prospects were tempting enough to take a trip to K.C. to review the market. We moved the company, several months later, to Northwest Missouri. I was 23 years old.

Nearly a year later I married in a civil ceremony, since I had become inactive in Church. She was also inactive and showed no desire to attend. I was attracted to her lack of interest in religion. I invited it.

Two years later our first daughter was born. My parents began the indoctrination about an "eternal family" that could only happen through temple ceremonies. We gradually began attending services which eventually would lead to fulfilling my parents' wishes. I began studying the doctrine of my religion again in depth five years after returning from the mission field. Again I silently questioned what I was learning.

Time passed rapidly and I began breaking away from the family construction and woodworking business. I enjoyed making my own decisions without having to consider the finances and personal challenges of other family members. I still loved them but did not want to know about all facets of their lives, also, Samoa was still in my heart and mind and had not faded after seven years, and now, also, with three daughters I wanted them to experience life, culture, and customs different from that of the Midwest.

Like Coming Home

Work had been going well and there was money in the bank. I treated my spouse to a three island tour of Hawaii while the grandparents cared for the girls. I still remember the energy that pulsed through me as I stepped off the aircraft in Honolulu. I had never been so affected by a place the way I was affected at that moment. I couldn't put it into words at the time. It was like setting foot on sacred ground. Like coming home to a place I had known and had a great attachment to. I had not, to that date, ever felt so welcomed.

All during the trip I had such a longing to move my family there and knew that if it was to be, the doors would open and it would be realized.

We returned home to Missouri. It was so wonderful to see the children again. I told my parents of the great experience we had but nothing to any one of my desire to live there. I knew within myself that it would be a stepping stone to the fulfillment of a future experience I would have in Samoa as the doors of opportunity would reveal themselves.

Hawaii

Upon discussing it with my spouse, she agreed we should leave the area and 'step out on our own' where we could be away from the loving family influences that tended to limit opportunities for our own growth. I knew she would much rather move to Utah to be near her family but she agreed we needed to be away from all family members and that there was great strength in bonding more within our own little family unit. I was grateful for her input at that time. We agreed to move our family to Hawaii.

We had returned from our vacation just prior to Christmas 1978. In March 1979 we auctioned most of our belongings, rented the house and sold the vehicles.

My wife would go on to Utah with the girls to visit her parents while I went on to Hawaii to arrange for an apartment, buy a car, and look for work. She would meet me two weeks later in Honolulu.

I greeted my little family at Honolulu International Airport. The first words I was greeted with from my spouse was that she thought of staying with the children in Utah. I told her I was glad she didn't. The 'Utah syndrome' in young people raised there has caused many, many divorces. Many young girls raised there are beguiled by the protection they feel in the Utah Valley at the foot of the Wasatch Mountain Range. I had witnessed it many times in other couples as well as in my own marriage.

After settling in our apartment in Makaha we began enjoying the Polynesian people and their lifestyle. I would eventually find my way to Laie being hired by a mainland construction company who had been contracted to build the new sports complex on the BYU-Hawaii campus. I became Lead-man on the project. I had 44 workers on four crews, the majority of Samoan and Tongan nationality. Samoans and Tongans have been, and still are, great rivals. They did not tend to work well together.

Everyone was surprised. We had a great relationship and enjoyed working together. The project was ahead of schedule.

Just prior to the groundbreaking I met with the head of the construction arm of the church for the Honolulu office. He was aware of my international experience with my parents in Uruguay and Guatemala as a youth. He assured me that my construction background, and having lived overseas was of interest and that he would keep me in mind.

Chapter 5

Samoa!

Six months into the project on campus I received a call from the Hawaii Director. He told me about the territory he was responsible for. It included Hawaii, Micronesia, Guam, Tahiti, Samoa, Tonga, New Caledonia, Vanuatu, Solomon Islands and other smaller Island nations. They were looking for someone with my experience to head up a project for them in one of the Island countries. I told them I would love to serve in whatever capacity I could. The Director said, "Brother Allen, we'd like to offer you a superintendent position on the Islands of Samoa."

I had done all I could, from a personal level, to place myself in a position where the fulfillment of this dream would be realized. I accepted the assignment. My family would be able to experience new cultures and customs along with me.

I informed my superiors at the project under construction. They told me they were disappointed at the prospect of loosing me but understood how important it was to assist the people of Samoa. I informed the crews and was very surprised when three of the workers approached me at the end of the day to tell me they wanted to return to their homes in Samoa to work under my direction. They said they had never worked with someone so caring about all of them yet with such a knowledge of construction. They wanted to learn all they could from me. I was humbled. I was honored. I told them that they should follow their dreams. They had immigrated from Samoa for an education. If they were to return to Samoa then that opportunity would open up for them. If not, they should continue with they're education while remembering the closeness we experienced in our workplace and perpetuate it wherever life would take them.

I signed an employment contract to oversee a construction project in the South Pacific Islands of Samoa. I was on my way from Hawaii with my family.

Upon our arrival I met with my boss and was informed of the project I was to be in charge of. I was to construct, with my crews, an assembly table to prefabricate the first church building of its kind in the islands for a local village. I would have complete charge of the project including the finances. It was a small budget of $80k U.S.

The project was flying. The crews were excited to learn a new form of construction and all was within budget. The wall sections were constructed first then hauled to the sight. Next the trusses. A separate crew had excavated and poured the foundation and slab in preparation for the erection phase.

The walls and trusses were installed, the roofing applied and the painting phase began. The excitement within the community was infectious.

Fiafia

The Samoan people were so gracious and loving to us and supported our family in every way. We were invited to many Fiafia's

(Samoan Luau's), at times we were the guests of honor. Wonderful Island food cooked in earth covered barbecue pits, socializing with the villagers who would always break into their Indigenous song and dance. They new how to party . . . Samoan style! We clapped and hummed to the tunes being sung in the local dialect. It was infectious. One of the dancing villagers would approach, inviting me to break into dance with them while those seated on woven mats and Tapa cloths laughed and cheered at my attempts to learn their moves. It was hilarious. Eventually, my wife and daughters would join in. We were all learning to celebrate Samoan style.

The Islanders would not only show us how to celebrate but also how to work. They showed great dedication in everything they did. A great example with a wonderful approach to life. The construction projects were all completed within budget and established time frames. My Samoan assistant was a great support and we had a wonderful relationship.

I had contracted a local architect to assist me in changing flaws in the designs sent from U.S. Headquarters. They expected us to construct church buildings designed to handle the elements in and around Utah, a desert area, with less than one-fourth the rainfall of Samoa. One of the first things I noticed upon arriving and inspecting the already constructed churches and schools, was the sagging, and in some instances, already fallen rain gutters throughout the Islands.

We raised the roof pitch design to accommodate the more than 150 inches of rainfall per year. We increased the window openings to allow more air flow in the tropical country. The buildings took on a more Samoan flavor. The locals were very supportive of the new changes. It was a good move.

Chapter 6

Fiji!

We were in Samoa for nearly a year when I was offered a promotion that included a move to the Islands of Fiji. The new position would include responsibilities regarding all aspects of real estate, materials management, construction and operations and maintenance. My territory would include New Caledonia, Vanuatu, Solomon Islands, and Tarawa along with Fiji. I would work hand in hand with the Finance Manager. The work was going well. After a year we returned to the States for a thirty day home leave.

Back in the U.S. for almost a month of vacation, just three days before we were to return to Suva, the Salt Lake City office called me in for some additional training. Upon my arrival I was informed that the Fiji office had been set on fire and that there was substantial damage. They were told that vandals had broken in and set fire to the office.

I called my assistant in Fiji and asked for more information.

"They called off the investigation!" His voice apologetic.

"Why?" I was upset.

"The finance manager called it off stating that the church didn't want any negative publicity," he said.

When I arrived 4 days later I inspected the burned out office. I was not allowed to reactivate the investigation.

In the few weeks prior to my return from home leave the responsibility for the overseeing of the

Fiji office was transferred from Hawaii to the New Zealand Area Office.

A few days later the New Zealand Area Comptroller arrived with the Director. They met with the finance manager then with me.

"You've done a great job here, Robert. I feel it best to not rock the boat any further with the investigation. We don't want to portray the church in a negative light"

"We already are by not clearing our own names. I recognize your position and will respect it." He proceeded to tell me he would be looking for a place in the Hong Kong Area Office for a transfer when I completed my contract in Fiji.

We were in Fiji for two years. While there, our son was born. For the next vacation I took the family to New Zealand, rented an RV and toured the North Island. It was a wonderful experience and I met so many great people along the way. I thought about immigrating there one day.

It is a challenge at the very least to uproot ones wife and children and move them nearly half way around the world. It can be very difficult for the spouse. Children adapt easier, at least mine did. Fortunately my wife did as well. It doesn't matter how talented a man is or how educated he is in his field, if the woman can not adapt then the man can not succeed in this type of environment.

It was my desire to serve and show others love, and make a difference in the world. To introduce my family to other cultures. To show them that we are all one family. To do unto others. I feel it was a tremendous success. It was worth working in a religiously controlled environment because people remember me more for who I am and what I did to help them more than the church I attended. Mormonism is the same as other religions in that there are those in control that demand respect and wield much authority. Then there are those that just try to love one another no matter what the cost or obstacle because they see the divinity in Creation.

Are You Willing?

I had a very profound experience while in Samoa before transferring to Fiji. I had been deep into meditation. I had seen leaders, revered for so many years, make choices that would negatively affect the direction of their future. Ones who had pulled the wool over peoples eyes for so long. I couldn't put the two together.

If the church was filled with prophets, seers and revelators, why couldn't they see what was going on. If one looks deeply enough in the paperwork of any construction project discrepancies will reveal themselves. I thought, naively, that most people were just like me. I certainly expected it from a construction arm of the church responsible for the distribution and expenditures of the sacred funds of tithing. The ten percent demanded by the church of all its membership. A tithe financially difficult for a large majority of the members but all the more given in faith that it would be of service to others throughout the world in the construction of churches and temples.

I was struggling with my conscience. I held myself and my family to a high standard of honesty. I knew I wasn't perfect, yet I also knew I would not misuse those sacred funds.

I went home during my lunch hour one day. I was alone in the house. I went into the bedroom, knelt down and began to pour out my heart, my concerns and frustrations. Not only was I struggling with what was going on at the office, I was struggling with my own beliefs in my religion. I had studied it for years and was concerned with many of the prophecies that members are demanded to accept as the literal word of God.

I spoke out in a firm voice, "I want to know the truth!"

"I want to have answers about these things!" I said it with a voice of conviction.

"Are you willing to pay the price?" asked an audible voice.

"Yes," I said, without hesitation.

Again the voice said, "Robert, are you willing to pay the price?"

Again I answered, "Yes!"

There was nothing more. I was left to the silence that followed. These words represented more than a response to my supplication. They caused me to be more introspective. To become more intuitive. To open up my mind, Spirit and Heart to further knowledge. Did I really mean what I had just said?

New Challenges

I felt at times that I was pioneering, stepping out on the edge but I also felt I was destined to experience what I was going through. I felt a loving hand showing me the way. Although I had experienced manipulation by some in charge, I was meeting wonderful people along the way. Humble, caring and loving people. Among the most gentle and loving of Fijians I had met was my Assistant.

Upon completion of my contract I returned to SLC with my family. I went directly to the office and asked to speak to the department in charge of my transfer.

Discovering that I had been misled about a transfer to another assignment, the Salt Lake City Headquarters informed me that they had nothing available in any other Areas at that time. They told me that I would possibly be contacted in the future when a position became available.

I was guided by my own intuitiveness to look for employment with a construction engineering firm in Ogden, Utah. It took about six weeks and I began working for them in July. I would manage construction projects in Utah and Southwestern Wyoming. I had as many as five projects under way at one time. I enjoyed the work. I received a decent salary and was assured three percent of the profit on each project brought in on, or below budget. I never saw the latter even though all my projects earned a profit.

Each project had its challenges. My superintendents were very experienced and helped me keep the projects on time and within budget. I was very busy and on the road daily during the week when my spouse informed me we were expecting a baby.

A New Addition

I was pleased and excited for our little family. The children were equally excited. We would ask them to choose the name for their new baby sister. They chose Laura Nicole. She would complete our family. They were so calming to my Soul. They still are to this day. I would disappoint them severely in removing myself from the church nine years later. I'm sure they felt at times that I didn't love them enough to stay in the church, when to the contrary, I left to find my own way clear of the manipulation of doctrine I saw in it from the time I was very young. I felt I was leading the way for them to eventually find their way out of religion too. It was my way of showing them Unconditional Love that they have yet to understand.

As they begin to scrutinize the information in 'Lightstorm' they will begin to experience the level of Love I have always had for them. They are an important part of my journey and I know in my Soul that I am an important part of theirs. We will, one day, all reunite and express our feelings and Love for one another without any interference from religion. With a profound understanding of Consciousness, of true Unconditional Love, of our connection to the Cosmos.

The Timing Was Perfect

I left my office and headed home for the evening. As I entered the house my spouse told me I had received a call from the Hawaii Church Construction Office. I returned their call. They wanted me to accept a contract to head construction in Micronesia. We would be headquartered in Guam for the year and a half or two year period. They further said they would clear it with the Salt Lake City Office if I was interested. We agreed to talk the following day.

My desire to work in the Islands of the Pacific was strong. My desire to be employed by the church again was much less. My parents had gone through some disappointments. I myself could attest to the very same although I went into it with my eyes open having seen their disappointments. I went within my heart and asked Higher Consciousness what I should do. The answer was, "you already know"... I did know. The timing was perfect.

The following day I received a call from the SLC Office stating their disappointment for the Hawaii Office calling me without consulting them first. They mentioned they were considering me for a three year contract in South America. They explained that the Director from Bolivia was in town and wanted to interview me. I told them I would like to meet him especially after the ordeal I went through in the Pacific.

It was a good interview. He seemed to be a gentle man. Well educated and directed toward helping others. I said nothing of my distaste for religion. I knew I needed to 'bite my tongue' and just do my job if they hired me.

I returned home to discuss the days events with my spouse. I didn't know how she would feel about another move overseas. She responded favorably. She told me she felt a need to get away from her Utah family the same way I felt in Missouri before moving to Hawaii. The following day the Director from Bolivia called to invite me for another round of interviews. I went with my spouses blessing.

I met with the Director first then filled out the necessary forms before meeting with the legal staff who wanted to review my previous employment record before presenting me with the three year contract. The contract was signed.

Chapter 7

Bolivia!

I flew down to La Paz, Bolivia to review my responsibilities with the Director that interviewed and hired me. Three days later I received a phone call from my Father telling me my Mother had been hospitalized for an emergency operation. The operation was traumatic and she did not fare well. She slipped into a coma and was not responding. Her system was shutting down. My father told me that if she didn't respond by the next day he would, at her previous request, take her off life support.

Hanging up the phone I immediately went within. I asked what I should do, should I catch a flight that afternoon or wait? I heard my Mothers voice, "You are where you are supposed to be right now. We will always be connected, keep doing what your heart tells you." My heart told me I was in the right place and to follow the counsel she had given me. She passed on the following day and I returned to the U.S. to be present with my family at her funeral. I felt no grief at her passing, only joy! The tears I shed were tears of gratitude to her, for dedicating herself to her family and never showing favoritism, only love to each of us.

We prepared for the move to La Paz. I went in to SLC Headquarters for training in between packing for the movers. My spouse and five children and myself left Salt Lake International Airport for Miami. After arriving there we walked from one end of Miami International Airport to the other. More than a mile pushing carts with luggage and extra cargo along with five children. We received many strange looks but could get no assistance from any airport baggage handlers. We made the flight on time and had many wonderful helping hands to meet us in 'El Alto' at La Paz.

My first priority was turning around a construction program that was hemorrhaging. There was a huge need for new church buildings throughout Bolivia. The consensus before I had arrived was to continue with an 'in-house' program. The cost per square foot was at $65us. This was nearly double the cost of projects completed in the Brazil Area during the same period.

After reviewing the history of my new department I informed the Regional Director that I would use a format from my projects in the States, i.e. Interview, qualify and invite Bolivian construction firms I felt able to embrace an AIA(American Institute of Architecture) program after having adapted it to the needs and requirements of the construction industry within Bolivia. It was a good move. This allowed me to open dialog with government regulators who invited me to assist them in modifying and improving the industry in Bolivia without stepping on any toes. They saw that I wanted to use their successful Ideas as well, incorporated with the AIA program to elevate the quality of labor, control, and materials purchased from local manufacturers whenever available. Those materials not available locally could be purchased in Brazil not in the US like others had done before me.

This new concept and direction was exciting to put into effect. It was exciting to all but some diehard individuals who saw the potential to 'milk' the system slip through their hands. The Director called me into his office to review his concerns.

I reminded him, "You hired me and brought me here to rescue this program. What has happened in the past has been costly. I'm here to resolve the situation, which can be done if you do not tie my hands." I respected him as my boss and did not waste words about the needed direction.

He showed me by his actions and support that we were going to be very successful. He upheld my decision and further helped me in my success by assigning the US ex-patriot architect that had been working directly under him, to now work under me. It was an inspired move.

We worked together on plans and specifications for seven different types of buildings that would be harmonious in villages, towns, and cities from 16,000 feet up in the Andes, down to 300 feet elevations in the Amazon Basin. Even in a small country like Bolivia we were working on concepts and designs within each region. Bolivia had many cultural and regional differences.

Along with the Architectural Department and the Engineers within it, I had an Assistant Engineer and three Multi-project Engineers. We eventually qualified seventeen General Contractors and after putting thirty-three projects out for bid ended up contracting all of those qualified.

Some of the bids came in under our projected costs and rather than put unneeded financial burden on the contractor to perform when there was a potential underestimation of certain items in the contract, I negotiated an adjusted contract amount where they would make more than their originally budgeted profit. It made for a great relationship between us but still remained within our budgeted amount.

All thirty-three projects were initiated within a four week period. There were more than 100 workers on each project. It was the largest construction venture in Bolivia at the time. All projects came in on schedule and within budget. The cost was in excess of $18m. We took the quality of construction to a new level and the entire country was proud of our accomplishment, even those who didn't like the religion. We reduced the cost per square foot by 50%.

Putting My Ego Aside

We had been in Bolivia for a year when I was called into the office of the Stake President in La Paz. I sat down facing him at his desk. We chatted briefly then he calmed his voice and said,"The First Presidency (Mormon Prophet and Counselors), has asked me to extend the Ordination of Bishop to you for the Calacoto Barrio near where you live."

I wasn't completely surprised. I didn't respond immediately. I hung my head as tears welled up in my eyes. He was thinking I was humbled and moved at the calling. I knew what was involved and I knew I did not want any ecclesiastical responsibility. I was adhering to church obligations to maintain a valid contract with the Church and the Construction Department. I had been keeping my feelings about the religion to myself. I had been hiding them for many years, but what would I say now? . . . My head bowed with tears in my eyes, I went within, "What shall I do?" I said. Then the words from the 'Ancients' . . . "accept the calling!", I raised my head, looked the Stake President in the eye and accepted.

I had communicated with the 'Ancients' many times over the years. I had asked the same question multiple times in the past, "How long do I have to remain in this religion?"

The answer remained the same, always, "You will know when it's time. There will be no doubt. In the meantime observe, learn all you can. This is an important time in your destiny."

I disliked my religion. I loved the members of my congregation. They were so loving in return. An ex-patriot member of the congregation approached me one Sunday immediately after services and said, "Bishop Allen, my husband and I have seen the church in action in many countries since we work within the US Embassy Program. I want to tell you that I have never seen a Bishop demonstrate the level of Love you show us as your flock." She hugged me and walked away. I couldn't speak. My heart was in my throat. I thought, "What wisdom! The 'Ancients' have never misled me."

I was careful as I prepared my sermons. At times I would be given a theme from SLC. I would not write anything down or read from notes to the congregation. From the time I was eleven years old, I had followed the instructions I was given by whom I would come to find out, were the 'Ancients'.

A Loving Voice

It was 1959 and I had accepted an assignment to give an inspirational talk in Sunday School to the congregation where we lived in Spokane, Washington. I was extremely shy and most people who knew me expected me to back out. I didn't.

I prepared my own talk, asked for no help from my parents and the next Sunday morning stood before several hundred people and delivered my message, looking down at times in my nervousness to my notes hoping not to make a fool of myself and cause my peers to find fault with my presentation.

I was surprised that everything went well. After the service many members approached me shaking my hand, hugging me, and patting me on the head. They were more amazed than me and I was walking on air. My head must have looked twice its' size from the pride I felt.

We lived just two blocks from the church building. I began walking home. As I crossed the main street in front of the building, feeling so satisfied with myself, someone spoke to me in a loving voice, but I was alone. The voice said, "There will never be a need to prepare a sermon. The words you will say will be put on your lips," then silence.

As Bishop of the Calacoto Ward in La Paz, Bolivia, twenty-four years later, I would stand before my congregation weekly, lower my head and await the message. I still do it to this day.

Ahead of Schedule

The construction program was so successful that my three year contract was fulfilled in less than two years. I could have remained in Bolivia for another year but felt it would not be the honest way to proceed. I asked if there was somewhere to transfer to for the remainder of my contract. Nothing was available. I announced that I would return to the States and not waste the churches tithes while completing my final year. I was excited to move on to the next phase of my life.

Returning to the US we eventually settled back in the Midwest. I was not excited to move back to Missouri but felt it was necessary as I began distancing myself from the church preparing to leave it one day. I recall telling my spouse and other members of the family that I loved the gospel but hated the church.

Struggling With Religion

More than twenty years earlier when my father had committed to a long term contract with the same corporate arm we moved to Montevideo, Uruguay, where he supervised the construction of a large church building in the suburbs.

Six months into the project Dad was moved into a management position to oversee construction in all the Spanish speaking nations of South America where the church was growing. My mother, five sisters, and myself, saw very little of him from that time on until he left the corporate side of the Church five years later.

Even though I was just a teenager I saw my father struggle with the corporate attitude. The positioning of power on the temporal side, different from the ecclesiastical side of the church.

Dad was an excellent builder and was known for his integrity and quality of construction as a successful contractor in Spokane for twenty years prior to accepting the assignment to South America. He loved his family and wanted to lead by example in being a pioneer in the church construction program, and I am sure he intended to stay in there the rest of his professional life. He was a powerful example of dedication to a cause. His cause. In his desire to serve his God and Church and help others throughout the world.

He didn't speak any Spanish when we left for Uruguay, but within three months he was conversing with, and directing workers, and missionaries in their native tongue. I worked for him on the first project and learned the language myself. The difference was that I was 14 and dad was 42. It came natural for me but not for him. The older a person is, when beginning to learn another language, the more difficult it can be, especially for Americans who were not encouraged to learn other languages in the first place. It was another of the powerful lessons my father would teach me. The importance of dedicating yourself to good causes and fighting the good fight through to the end.

Oh, yes. The final words my father delivered to the Director upon leaving were, "I'd rather be on the outside paying my tithing than on the inside watching how it is being spent." I had difficulty fully agreeing with him. My thoughts were, "Why pay tithes at all when you were a first-hand witness to their misuse?" I kept silent.

This spirit of dedication in him was also the cause of much of his frustration and sorrow during the last 30 years of his life. What he expected from his Church was the same level of dedication to mankind that he had demonstrated throughout his life. He expected the same level of dedication from the Church that he showed the Church. He never saw it. He was very disillusioned and hurt by the actions of the organization that he loved and dedicated his life to.

I had often asked why situations occurred the way they did. My parents were so dedicated to living a good life by showing and teaching by example but there were often unexpected repercussions. My mother was a dedicated genealogist and relayed life stories she herself had experienced as well as those unearthed in her genealogical research concerning hardships in past generations on both sides of the family.

The Nature Of A Pioneer

We all go through challenges during our lifetime as well as do those who came before us. I would search for many years, reading the written words of many revered authors. I also sought answers within. Words that I read, rang true in my Spirit and stimulated Higher Consciousness, and assisted me in my awakening, were found in 'Path of Empowerment,' by Barbara Marciniak.

She addresses the drive we sometimes have to step out on the edge;

> "The very nature of a pioneer is to walk alone into new territory, to go where no one else has traveled. As a pioneer you must learn to be alone with your discoveries. During times of instability, all of your fears can come up. Your emotions can take you deeper and deeper into the realm of feeling, where courage and love are required to encounter the wounds you carry. When you choose the path of empowerment, there are times when you must deal with life on a very profound

level, and moments of despair can arise when you wish you simply did not know the bigger picture. Even the idea that ignorance is bliss can often appear appealing. This is a natural response because of the depth of emotional connections you are experiencing. Yet emotional states do not go on forever; the best and the most difficult are ephemeral and eventually slip away. Emotions can play you, and emotional depth is a captivating aspect of your human experience. When you choose the stance of a victim, someone or something else is always to blame for what happens to you. To really claim your mind and free your spirit, you must consider your personal attitude as well as the criteria you use to interpret your experience. Do you see life and all you encounter with the glass half-full or half- empty? Are you in charge of your mind, body, and spirit, or does someone else always have more authority? Can you detect the feelings that define and confine your experiences? A change of attitude stems from a change in how you see and interpret your role in life and all your experiences. New interpretations create new feelings, which in turn fertilize the field of energy for new experiences". (pages 128-129)

My father had given authority to the Church to instruct him on how he should live his life. He was told to have faith that he was doing right. Giving away his power to live a peaceful and productive life caused the confusion that he could not understand. Religion has never been the answer!

I Don't Understand

The last meeting I had with my father was 6 months after I left the church and had been excommunicated. We sat together in his little apartment in Nauvoo, Illinois, and talked.

"Dad, I love you so much," I said, with tears welling up in my eyes.

"I love you too, son," with tears in his eyes, too.

He had been shaken to the core as a result of my leaving the church. He didn't understand it but he had always known of the spiritual connection I had with heaven from the time I was a child.

"I don't know why this has happened and I'm sad that you don't want to be a Mormon, yet I feel there is something more than I can comprehend going on here. Maybe I'll know what it is one day." He hung his head.

"Dad, I can tell you that the joy I am experiencing in my life right now is something I could not find in any religion, let alone the one I was raised in. I am now my own guide. I am seeing my way through a clear, pure looking-glass. My love for you is stronger than ever. I am seeing deeper into the knowledge of The Creator. You're the one who encouraged me to seek Him with all my heart, and I have!" I said. I found that it could only be realized outside of religion.

As I said that, I felt the same feeling rush through me that I had in that strawberry patch when I was just a boy.

"I hear your words, son, and I see your passion, and I did teach you that, but I can't comprehend what you've done.

"You say you love the Lord but not the church. I can't separate the two. To me they are one and the same," he said, with his eyes filled with love for his youngest son, yet confusion in my separating the Lord from the religion.

"Dad, God is much more than religion. God is the reason I love you, not religion."

We embraced and kissed each other on the cheek, and I departed. It would be the last time I would see him. He would pass on 5 years later. He did tell one of my sisters just before he died that he didn't understand what had happened with me but that God knew and it would all be remedied in the end.

The Essence Of Human Experience

Marciniak continues;

'As strange as it seems, accepting more responsibility for being the creator of your experience frees you to explore the shadow side of life; without shadows, you would see very little of life . . . The essence of human experience is to participate in the full range of human expression; to learn how to navigate these unpredictable realms and to survive with your consciousness in alignment are some of the profound spiritual tests of the times. A deep inner knowing based on innocent trust is required to proceed on the path of empowerment. To swim and to dive deep into the immense pools of emotions, you must make the link between thoughts, feelings, and beliefs; otherwise, emotional energy can be a journey into madness where nothing makes any sense. When you consciously intend to investigate your feelings by being responsible for creating all of your experiences for a significant purpose, the resulting release of pent-up emotional energy can feel fantastic.' (pp 129-130)

I have found these word to be true in my life. I am the designer of my life. I set my own course. I, sooner or later, see the wisdom in my choices and how I allow them to move me in the direction of destiny.

Chapter 8

Leaving The Reality Of Religion Behind

I recall saying just before leaving religion that, 'If leaving the Church condemns me to hell then so be it.' I had been confused and questioning from my childhood. I couldn't stand to think of an eternity following those beliefs.

I would leave and follow my own path. In a worldly sense it would cost me dearly. I would experience the wrath of those I called my family and my friends.

I mistakenly thought they would understand my need to follow my own path. I was wrong. What we assume of others in our lives is quite often incorrect. I realized that unconditional love, as taught in and through religion, simply is not unconditional, it is very obviously conditional. I was loved and respected as long as I remained, but by leaving I was targeted and hated because I had rejected the teachings they hinged theirs lives upon. The fear of my leaving caused them to question why I would do such a dangerous thing, putting my eternal soul in jeopardy. Some questioned their own motives for remaining in religion and became more angry at me for causing them to bring up these questions and doubts in their own minds. They would become more dedicated to their religion in feeling guilty for having questioned it while evaluating my actions in leaving.

As I witnessed the suffering my actions had caused I was concerned. I had no desire to harm anyone, I simply had to follow my own path. I was learning more about the human experience than I had ever known before. I was seeing the reaction my leaving was causing and saddened by their lack of understanding, but I couldn't let them alter my choice and rule over the direction of my destiny.

Changing My Reality

As days, weeks, and months went by I realized I had left a 'reality,' one created by others and taught to me because they believed it to be true and from their god. I began creating a new 'reality' for myself. As time went by a clearer focus came into view. The reality of the religion I left was a reality within the much larger reality of all religion. All of them had their own gods whether eastern or western religions, they were all following the same directives from what they regarded as other higher sources.

If the higher sources of these organizations were gods, why were there so many? Why did proving themselves to their gods include wars, killing not only men but women and children as well as unborn baby's? All religions have been guilty! Even spinoffs of larger religions are guilty by association. While well intentioned people have denounced and apostatized from the main stream religions, they have remained within the reality of religion and continued worshiping the same god or gods worshiped in the organization they denounced. They have changed nothing. They have increased the reality of religion by diversification.

All of us are what we believe! We can be no different!

When one seeks truth and understanding all worldly conditioning has to be set aside. Religion and a belief in a god is included within worldly conditioning. It is all three dimensional. That explains why Unconditional Love does not exist within the organizations of this world, nor can it. Unconditional Love can only come through Consciousness, through the heart. As I have previously stated, Brilliance comes from somewhere outside the mind, likewise Unconditional Love comes from outside the human heart. It is Divine and can only come through Consciousness, which is Divine.

As I began the journey down my new pathway I erased the conditioning from the chalkboard of my mind. The chalkboard was empty and the conditioning it contained was put into storage and I could access it at will. It would not be allowed to force me in any direction. The storage room of my previous conditioning was not all bad. It contained some wonderful teachings I would draw upon as I began my path of discovery. (page 212 Deprogramming the internal computer)

Now You Teach Me!

One of the first things I did was to declare in a loud voice, "Now you teach me!" I didn't know who or what I was speaking to, I only knew it was not the god of any religion. I would not be disappointed. I would learn that the 'Ancients' had been the major source of my internal teachings all along the way.

The reality I was seeking, even creating, encompassed all worldly realities, but even more, it would include all of creation upon this Earth, throughout this Galaxy and Universe and extend to other Universes, all of creation!

I was shown a reality, in my own mind and thoughts, in the form of a circle becoming a sphere . . . a bubble. Within this particular sphere were all the teachings, beliefs, doctrines and commandments of my prior religion. I then witnessed it touching or connecting with other spheres, but not totally. There were connections with many other spheres, even Islam. Some of the doctrines of my religion included several of the doctrines of Islam, not commonly accepted in Christianity. Other spheres included hundreds of forms of Christianity including their creator gods. Each sphere represented its own reality.

All of the connected spheres were shown within the larger sphere of religion. I saw another sphere encircling smaller spheres of politics, administrations, governments, corporations and even family organizations of power along with their creator gods. This second large sphere was connecting with the sphere of religion.

Both of the large spheres were swallowed up into an even larger one. This was named Third Dimension Frequency. All embraced by 'Free-Will.'

I would begin seeing more with my spiritual vision, many of the other creations and entities around this Earth and throughout our Solar System and beyond, all outside the spheres of reality but certainly, unconditionally, connected to Source. I would also be able to photograph them and interact with them and the message of Love they bring and represent. Most have been of a higher dimension, Spiritual. I have photographed some physical craft from time to time, but my desire is to commune with higher Consciousness, higher dimensions. We are what we attract . . . we attract what we are.

There are some benevolent entities in our dimension and they will reveal themselves to those who seek understanding and knowledge through Consciousness. As they do, one understands their need to mask their presence in frequencies other than the ones we live in. They can even appear to us in their crafts but you will recognize the difference, they will not deceive, they will radiate a vibration of peace and Love . . . all others encompass fear, question, doubt, power, intimidation, and control.

There is a need to address the malevolent because it also exists in this dimension. It is masked by fear, it is motivated by fear. Malevolence loves to intimidate, control, and direct world energy. Those involved in the deception are able to move in and out of frequency, appearing and disappearing at will. Religions have been created through their manifestations. Wars have been declared and fought, and still are. Their efforts have had devastating effects and caused much turmoil and suffering throughout world history, and it continues to this day.

Involved in the malevolent we find 'entity possession.' Again, we are what we attract. Fear is the key. The greatest teaching we as humans can practice is Love. Fear cannot control when Love is present. Entity possession is not the ideal. They will come in because they have been invited. Once invited they will take over as much as they are allowed to. In our lazy Western culture it is in epidemic proportion. Entity possession is not the same as demonic possession. Entity possession is much more prevalent and easier to do something about. All one has to do is get up off the sofa, put down the remote and physically do something that makes you feel better and follow through with good goals, respecting yourself, then focusing that attention you have acquired, through your efforts, into compassion and love for others.

We inhabit a physical body, it teaches us. We must allow Consciousness to teach the body. We first must love ourselves, unconditionally. Religion has taught us to lose ourselves in the service of others. This allows us to gain respect of ourselves, but Unconditional Love has to be allowed in before we can do anything divinely effective.

In all candor, I have had to evaluate myself from time to time. There have been many occasions when I have felt the presence of Supreme Creator, Source, in my life. At other junctures I had to do a reboot as I discovered a lack of respect and even love for myself that I found was do to outside influences I had allowed in. As I go within I am able to correct the situation through Consciousness first, then allowing that perfect energy to counsel my emotions. I find myself back on track.

I was comfortable criticizing other religions throughout my religious life, then I included my own upon leaving it, but, as I entered into my new reality I was shown that I was not deceived nor lied to as I claimed. I was taught that each reality creates its own truths. Within my former religions' teachings I was a son of perdition. Within the religion of my family and religious friends that statement is true because it was included in the teachings of that one reality. As a religious individual passes on to the next dimension he or she is welcomed by those who have gone on previously with like beliefs. They enter into families of like believers, I call them 'communities'. The same community one embraces in this life continues after death because that reality includes the afterlife. The individual remains in this community until there is a type of awakening and they begin questioning that reality. All those in the community eventually move forward upon being shown the truth of life in the third dimension and the deceptive teachings and conditioning they chose to accept and follow having exercised their own free-will.

Sin, heaven, hell, punishment and salvation only exist within the reality of religion. Heinous acts and crimes performed within that reality can activate a Universal counsel of justice that arrives at a form of punishment, together with the individual, and the guilty party then oversees its own punishment, perhaps isolation and a form of reprimand including an incarnation involving the same form of victimization caused by him in his previous incarnation, becoming a victim of his own making.

Most of us have incarnated to this Earth to follow good teachings and live exemplary lives. I have found that losing oneself in the service of others is most effective after you first pay attention to yourself. Going within causes one to focus on the hearts desires and with some assistance from loving Guides, Masters, and Teachers, they help show us the value and wisdom of living in our own vibration, not in someone else's.

The Bakery

I went shopping one Thursday afternoon near the project I was working on. As I wandered through the bakery department I looked up and saw someone looking at me. It was a familiar face but I couldn't remember from where. Those dark eyes penetrated mine. Something was happening. I felt like I was waking up from a long sleep and seeing a new world. She would become the warrior I needed at my side.

I needed support in the separation from my children. I needed to be sustained in the war that was about to begin. I needed to be a warrior. The Ancients had helped me weather some very difficult storms in the past. I found I was also surrounded by many other warriors to assist me in the battle.

The timing was divine. It was no coincidence. A whole new world would open up to my view. A world of interdimensional support and Love.

A Condemned Man

It would take me some time to work through the anger and disappointment I felt as I was treated like a condemned man, but I was naive and should have known to expect it. The target of well organized propaganda by some zealous church members, and other more vile stories and myths created by other members of my own family. All only having their origin in fear.

What angered me most was the constant barrage and indoctrination of my children and being unable to defend myself and continue to show them my Love. I could only go within my heart and Love my children no matter what they thought of me now. I felt pity and disgust for those attacking.

Within 6 weeks of my leaving the church I received an official document informing me that I had been excommunicated. I admit that I was nervous at the time since I didn't have a clear mental vision of what my future would be, only a deep feeling that I was on course with my destiny and that my heart and words would be felt by many people throughout the Earth. I had received glimpses of it at times during my life leading up to that moment but was unsure that I was really on the right path. I needed not doubt myself.

The one thing I did know was that I could not find my answers in the religion. I was taught, as were all young church goers of my generation, that to walk away from the truth of the gospel was to commit spiritual suicide. It would destroy the eternal bond that tied my family together. Another indoctrination surely based in fear!

Heaven In The Midst Of War!

I now spent most of my time working on the project. I telephoned the new warrior in my life for some counsel. We began talking about our lives up to the day we met. She explained to me about a dream she had the night before. She said it was about us. I began telling her my feelings and the connection I felt between us. She knew everything about my soon to be ex-wife, about my Love for my children. I hadn't told her about the church.

She broke in at that point to tell me more about the dream. She said,"I was talking with someone who knew you and they told me something."

I listened intently.

"When they told me, I rose up in my bed, completely alert and blurted out the words, he's a Mormon!" She stated she had been completely caught off guard. I smiled then went on to tell her the rest of my story. She was relieved to know that I was out of the church.

We talked on the phone every evening. We knew there were much higher powers at work in bringing us together.

At a prearranged time I took her out to dinner. We had gone to dinner before but we both new this would be the night of fulfillment, of following through with what was in our hearts and the beginning of an important phase in both our lives.

I had never talked to her about my journey during the night when I was 18. About the beautiful young girl I had made love to in that attic bedroom. As I began to share the experience her eyes came alive, she said, "it was you!" Then she told of her experience that same night.

She had gone to her Grandmothers house. She had been invited to spend the night there. Her special place was the bedroom in the attic. That night she too went into a deep sleep…I came to her. What she would further explain was that we were together in other places. She would be referring to other dimensions. We knew our connection was one through many lifetimes. My understanding of frequencies and dimensions was beginning to awaken. We both witnessed a heightened field of Energy to and from those dimensions and frequencies when we were together. Our own psychic abilities magnified and we sensed family members and other loved ones, who had passed on, around us frequently. We smelled my mothers perfume on occasions.

She had gone through much trauma in her childhood and teenage years. She learned how to escape her abuser by leaving her body. She would rest beneath a beautiful tree in a lush green field. She told me she could feel the most heavenly breeze brush against her face while there. When her abuser left she would return to her body.

I was moved beyond words. She was able to move in and out of dimensions to protect herself. I would be at her side when that individual would reappear in her life. I witnessed the power of letting go of the past, of refusing to be a victim, then embracing that guilt ridden person and forgiving. After thirty years of dealing with that guilt he was free. That beautiful woman had forgiven him. There was no doubt in my heart that we were together at this time because we had ordained it to be so. We would help and support each other during this phase of our lives.

Many times she would travel into other dimensions. Sometimes it would be during a restful break from the challenges of the day, but most of her journey's would begin as she reached a level of ecstasy while we were making Love. They were so intense that she would go to many other heavenly places ... places where she could rest and at times be taught. While there, messengers would greet me and bring messages through her, words of great Love and joy. My Mother came to me many times, speaking through that still body, and we would exchange our Love and at times reflect on experiences we had shared while she was still here in this dimension. She was close to me but also close to her and would appear to her from time to time. Her Grandmother would also appear to her and express her love and acceptance of me.

A Devious Conspiracy

I wouldn't discover it for another year, but at the very moment I left the church my brother had begun a campaign to discredit me in a way that I knew would one day come back to discredit him, even worse. He had communicated with the leadership of the church that I was going to attempt to assassinate their Prophet. Information concerning my vital statistics and background, including their reason for my excommunication, were sent to church leaders to be on the lookout.

The divorce proceedings took on a life of their own. Over a period of eleven months I would be put on the witness stand several times to respond to attacks and cross-examinations that were orchestrated by my brother and others determined to teach me how wrong I had been in leaving the church.

There would be a total of three judges to sit on the bench during that time. The second judge made no attempt to hide his dislike for me and made every effort to belittle and intimidate me. It was interesting to witness him turn a simple hearing for a divorce into a religious and political platform. My attorney kept shaking his head saying he had never seen anything like it before.

Almost a year had passed. Just days before what would be the final hearing, the judge was stricken with a heart attach and was hospitalized. My attorney told me the hearing was still on the calendar but he didn't know what to expect.

That next morning I drove from our home to the court hearing, a two hour drive.

A new judge was assigned and a new day dawned. The divorce was finalized in the newly appointed judges chambers, and in less than three hours the long ordeal was over. The divorce was final.

It would be the last I would see of my children for several years. They left for Utah the next day where their upbringing and mental and spiritual conditioning was easier to control and it became difficult for me to contact them for several years.

I often reflected on the experience I had in Samoa some years before when I was asked by the 'Ancients' if I was willing to pay the price, referring to my desire to have answers to my questions and my journey through life. I had no idea it would mean being isolated from my children that I loved so much, but the answer to that important question was still Yes! I have always felt that if I sought answers in my life even the harshest of experiences would, in the end, prove to be entwined with wisdom, joy, and fulfillment, and that it would effect the lives of my children for good even if they were kept from me for a period of years.

Chapter 9

A New Direction

Having left the religion of my ancestors behind, we moved into a new home. We were immediately welcomed into the community. We felt at home and made some wonderful friends. I spoke from time to time at local services, telling the story of my previous life and using some of my experiences to help uplift others facing unwanted obstacles in their own lives, encouraging them to stand strong, face the challenges, and find themselves victorious over any obstacle.

I learned through the experience with my previous religion that they were operating on a clear level of fear. Fear of me and the thoughts of what damage a 'Son of Perdition' could do to them locally and throughout the church. I realized I held power over them. They gave me that power. This was exactly what the creator gods hungered for, nourishment through fear. I ignored it. We went on with our lives. We even laughed to each other when the van of Mormon officials looking for evidence that would confirm their fears would appear in the neighborhood.

Some time had passed and I was approached by a group of individuals with a request to consider representing their ministry in Mozambique, Africa, where they were having devastating results attempting to set up a construction program using the local Pastors. They were wiring money to the locals in Malawi and not seeing results for their contributions. The head of the ministry would travel to Malawi and Mozambique every few months. They invited me to accompany them in the fall of the year to review the situation and give recommendations on how to move forward.

It was not difficult. I traveled with them to Africa, reviewed the situations there, then made my report. They needed to identify an individual to relocate to Africa for a specific time to administer funds, register the Ministry in Malawi, Mozambique, and Zimbabwe, identify and employ a local trustworthy PR representative, identify a location for a temporary headquarters until a permanent one could be built. During his time in Africa he would identify an individual who could assume the responsibilities allowing that Director to return to the US upon completion of his responsibilities.

On my initial visit to Malawi with the head of the ministry, the entire group was pleased with the way I related to the Malawians and how they interacted and responded to me. Prior to returning to the States, after two weeks, the head of the organization asked if I would accept the position as director in that area of Africa. I ultimately accepted the assignment and spent two years setting up the organization and identifying locals to oversee the program upon my return to the States.

A Lifetime Of Preparation

Prior to leaving for Africa, donating my services to a local church I had what others described as a near tragic accident as a large solid piece of concrete block, weighing more than eighty pounds fell from above my head and landed on the bridge of my right foot. I felt bones snap. There was some pain but what was more interesting was my reaction. My friend and coworker in this endeavor, felt terrible since he was the one who knocked the block loose. I thought of him and the look on his face as the heavy object fell, breaking my foot before I could move it.

I hobbled around for a minute. He wanted to take me to Emergency, immediately.

I spoke clearly, saying, "I'm scheduled to leave for Africa in two weeks. I don't have time for this injury!" I told him I would keep moving, working the remainder of the day, and I did. By the time I got home that evening I only showed a slight limp. I took off my shoe for the first time. My foot and ankle were already bruising. A compound fracture was obvious. We could see the broken bones underneath the stretched skin.

Under normal circumstances I would have gone to the Emergency Room but I also had been a witness to the intervention of Cosmic, Divine Energy in my preparation for Africa. I knew I was being watched over and that I, myself, was in a zone of protection and self-healing. I continued with my normal evening routine as though nothing serious had occurred. I took two aspirin before going to bed. I awoke twice in the night and evaluated myself. I would attempt to roll over on my left side then my right a couple of hours later. There was no pain in my foot, my leg nor any other part of my body. I thanked my Creator.

I slept peacefully through the night. I was at peace in my heart. I knew that nothing would interrupt this divine mission. One of dedication based in Love for others. I felt the uninterrupted protection from the moment I accepted the assignment and would continue to feel it throughout the next two years in Malawi, Mozambique, Zimbabwe, and South Africa.

I arose the next morning. I put the same shoe on my injured foot, laced it snuggly, prepared breakfast and left for work. My foot was gaining strength during the day and continued to do so over the next two weeks. The bone was returning to its' proper place. There was a knob like object covering the fracture. My foot, ankle, thigh and entire knee area became covered in colors ranging from brown, black, orange, yellow, purple and possibly other colors. It took weeks for my leg to return to its' natural skin tone. Any discomfort I felt completely disappeared after just three days. I have not had any pain in it since.

There is infinite life in infinite form throughout frequencies and dimensions. We are what we attract. I learned that our thoughts and especially our intent was more powerful than a damaged, even broken bone, and Energy, Light, and Love can be, and are, projected through frequency and dimension to support our own worthy intent. We are all connected to the Universe, to Prime Creator, to Source. The accident, then, was no accident. It was an event to validate what I had been feeling in the protective Energy that enveloped me and everything associated with that specific assignment.

Africa

Commitment Through Intent

I left St Louis for NYC., connected with the Ministry Head and his entourage for a fourteen hour flight to Johannesburg, South Africa. We would catch another flight the next day to Lilongwe, Malawi. I had been to many other countries in the Western Hemisphere but this was my first contract to Africa.

I witnessed people in their seemingly poor state, by US standards, happier than most first world citizens. Why were they so content when they had nothing of possessions compared to us? I understood! I had my focus on helping the people of Africa rather than falling victim to our own synthetic, shopping mall oriented culture. The village people of Malawi and Mozambique were at home in their mud stuccoed, thatched roof huts interacting with their children, their source of pride. Truly precious jewels in their crowns. Children are the most important possessions in the villagers life.

I went with the objective of helping them but quickly realized that I was also the student. I did help them build churches and schools where they could gather in friendship as a community. Most of them accepted me and became very good friends. No matter where you go in the world one will find much prejudice and justification to belittle and tear down what Love attempts to grow. Some of the leaders took on a more aggressive approach to me. They could see the financial advantage to being an appointed ecclesiastical leader. A few, unfortunately, became 'westernized.'

We had completed a church building, a school classroom wing, and a pastors house in Malawi. Everything in the village was lit by kerosene lamps or candles in the evening. The Pastor asked to meet with me on my swing through that area inspecting other projects under construction. The complex had been completed a few weeks prior to my visit and all was in use accept the pastors residence. I met with him and his board of Elders and was told directly to install electricity to his house. I told him it was not included in the project funds especially when there was no power readily available in that area of the town. He told me he would not move into the home until it had electricity. I looked him directly in the eye and taught him something about what it truly meant to be a pastor.

"To be a pastor is to humbly lead. The only way to do that is to first become a servant to your congregation, gaining their love and trust and they will support you."

He responded with ice cold eyes, "You are white. You come from America. You must take care of us."

"You do not understand the calling you have." I could see I was getting nowhere. "You are setting an unworthy goal for your congregation to behold. If you believe you are called by God to lead these people then teach them about the law of tithing and raise the $4,000 dollars you need to bring electricity to your house that this Ministry has built for you out of its' desire to help, at no cost to you!" I left the meeting and headed to home to Tete, Mozambique.

The Whirlwind

On another trip to Malawi I went to a village on the outskirts of Lilongwe for a Sunday service. I was asked by their director to teach his congregation. The corrugated roofed structure with red earth stuccoed walls was packed. The pews were made of rough sawn planks supported by two narrow stumps, one at each end. The floor was made of packed red dirt that had been watered down to make it harden as it dried. The podium was elevated about 6 inches and was made the same way. As I entered the structure I could barely find space to walk. People were sitting on the hard mud packed floor since the rough plank pews were filled. I followed Joseph, the Director, to the front. We sat down and began to sing with the little congregation. African voices raised in praise to their God is a wonderful experience to behold. It is a sound unique to Africa.

After two or three songs Joseph began by addressing his flock. I stood as he introduced me. It is a marvelous sight to see when you are the only white person in a group of native Africans. Their bright white eyes and smiling happy faces welcoming you. There was an energy of Divine Love present there that day.

As we looked out over the congregation everyones attention was drawn to the main door, as it flew open, and a small whirlwind entered the church, proceeded up the narrow center isle, turned right toward a side entry, the door swung open and the whirlwind exited the building. The Universe confirmed that day that I was in the right place. There were 258 souls present and we were all one family.

With the ministry registered in the three countries and construction underway for the new headquarters I turned the responsibilities over to a local qualified person and returned to the States.

Changes

There are challenges in every relationship. We don't always know what our spouse is going through. I have always felt that each person needed to find their own way in this life. I have always stayed clear of making an important decision for someone else, including my spouse, but, I have always tried to support the decision made believing it was in the persons best interest in assisting in the learning process of each individual. I have had many people throughout my life ask me what they should do or decide. I have always tried to turn the situation around in a way that they would end up answering their own question. There were times when my spouse would confront me. I was never very good at arguing. I would get frustrated because I would not be able to coordinate my words in response to the argument. I remember thinking that I needed to figure out how to remain calm at those moments.

I felt my spouse struggling inside.

My feeling was that some of the challenges we face in our youth resurface if we invite them. What

I came to understand soon after was that our time together in this dimension was coming to an end.

I remember finding myself in another of those situations. I didn't know what to say. I went inward to see if I could effectively counter what was happening. I clearly remember separating from my body, stepping to my right side and observing both of us at the same time. She was speaking and was expecting a response similar to other occasions.

As I observed I noticed I was feeling no emotion, and with that I was able to formulate a response out of wisdom. I learned how to respond appropriately in that moment. I stepped back into my body and spoke, softly, quietly. She could not respond. The discussion was over. We hugged each other and spent the remainder of the day together. It was a good outcome.

She went to her special place on the other side. Suddenly a voice. It was coming through her but it clearly was not her.

"Hello, Robert."

"Hello," I said. "Who is this?"... No answer, then...

"You are both greatly Loved and watched over," said the voice.

It seemed we were not progressing on a spiritual or personal level as a couple. Our relationship was stagnant. We both felt like we were spinning our wheels and getting nowhere.

"What's happening? I would like some answers," I said in a determined voice.

The response, "Are you ready?"

I answered quickly, "Yes!"

The voice repeated the question, "Are you ready?"

'The Ancients' were speaking. They always repeated themselves when talking to me, but left the remainder of the message to what I would soon experience.

I answered again, "Yes!"

They departed, and a few moments later she returned having heard nothing of the conversation.

I told her what they said. We both wondered what it meant.

Things were not improving. We were not communicating well. She left and wouldn't return for three weeks. When she did return I didn't pressure her for information. She was clearly different. By the end of January she came into my office and said it was over. Our relationship had come to an end.

I sat looking at her, waiting for more explanation. I realized what the 'Ancients' were referring to.

It seemed unfortunate that our relationship would unravel. I had questions, and doubts about myself.

Looking To Head South

I had wanted to move South for many years, in fact, we had planned moving to Florida when the finances would permit. Now, things had changed. I began thinking about Bolivia and the success I had there. I began attempting to track down the engineers and local architects I had worked with in an attempt to relocate to South America when the divorce was final.

I was doing some real soul searching. I didn't have a clear picture in my mind of what had happened. The teachings would come over time. I would be taught about relationships of an interdimensional nature. I have always felt that the process of marriage was more controlled by religion and the passion of relationship and true dedication has taken a back seat to religions demands.

I was on the right track.

Relationships

"Marriage in the world is based on religious dogma. Religions' demands and specific commandments control that type of relationship." The 'Ancients' were speaking.

"Marriage is a contract originally established by the church. Religion has it confused purposely. It is true that there is no marriage in heaven, in other words, in higher dimensions. There is no need for it because all inhabitants of higher dimensions are directed by and through Love. If there is an intimate relationship between individuals there, the commitment is mutual with the knowledge that all are connected to Source. All is Love and all expressions are valid within the higher dimensions. The world does not comprehend the act of Love at that level but those seeking and achieving Higher Consciousness will understand.

"As in your relationship, it continues in other frequencies and higher dimensions. You were brought together at a specific time and place, in this lifetime, on this Earth, to accomplish precisely what you did. You were to leave the indoctrination of your ancestors and she was there to give you the strength and support you needed that you could not provide for yourself. Your part in the relationship gave her strength she could not provide herself. It was an important event in her destiny, during this lifetime, to complete. When it was accomplished you both were required to move on to the next phase of experience on separate paths. This was agreed upon by both of you prior to your entrance into this mortality. Relationships are meant to teach. At times it takes several relationships within the same lifetime to complete the specific journey you are on."

The message was profound. I clearly understood it and felt a wonderful warmth come over me. I wanted her to be okay. They assured me she was.

Life went on and I was actively seeking a change of scenery to South America. I wasn't seeking another partner. I said to whoever was listening, "If there is another woman out there you're going to have to bring her to me because I won't be looking. You're going to have to prove it." I wondered what the next phase would be.

My Religion Is Love!

I logged on to a professional Latin American Architectural/Engineering web site looking for my associates from my contract in Bolivia. None of the those professionals were caught up in religion when I worked with them before. I couldn't locate them. Almost twenty years had passed. I wasn't surprised. I began looking in other countries, Guatemala, Brazil and Colombia. I was communicating with several engineers as well as attorneys, looking to get my foot in the door. I came across the profile of a University professor in International Business Administration. I sent a greeting. There was no response. About three weeks later I came across the same information and sent another greeting. This time there was a response. I explained my background and desire to return to South America. She informed me that she knew an engineer in Venezuela who was putting together a project in Aruba. We communicated almost daily and became quick internet friends. I remembered the message from the 'Ancients'. I was ready for whatever.

This took place early in May 2005. Two weeks later she informed me she was coming to Miami for her daughters wedding at the end of May. She had told her daughter about me and it was suggested she invite me to the wedding. I had to decline since I had some commitments with my work for that weekend. A few days later my clients informed me that they were going out of town for Memorial Day. My commitments were postponed to the following week. I emailed her of the change and accepted her invitation. She dedicated her time and efforts to putting her son through medical school. I wondered if this woman would become an important part of my future.

After attending the wedding and the reception I invited her to accompany me the next day, Memorial Day, on a drive to Key West. She accepted.

We left early that Monday and the closer we got to Key West the more traffic we saw. I realized I had not anticipated well, due to the Holiday weekend. We had been driving for nearly three hours and still had some miles to go. We decided to return to Miami, and, what would normally be a two hour drive turned into eight. We got into Miami at Midnight. We made use of the extra time and got to know each other better. She started calling me 'Papi,' a term of endearment. I liked it.

In all the years I had lived in Latin America I never thought of a relationship with a Latina. It had never come to mind, but I was drawn to her and her incredible ability to Love. She has been a true beacon of strength and Unconditional Love. She treats all people with respect and freely admits that her religion is Love.

In July I would travel to Venezuela and meet her at her sisters home in Caracas. We stayed there a week then flew to Barranquilla, Colombia, and her home. I had met her daughter through the wedding and was now about to meet her son. Both of her children are as loving as she is. They quickly became important in life and I thought of them as part of my family. Under the circumstances that still remain with my own children, I have much more contact with her son and daughter and love them very much.

I traveled back and forth to Colombia that year and finally, in December, she introduced me to her brothers. She had kept me under cover until then. Her sisters knew me and had accepted me instantly. Brothers are always protective of their sisters. She waited until we were engaged to reveal me to them. They were very accepting of me, I'm sure with some reservation. I would have felt the same.

The words of the 'Ancients' were constantly with me. I was getting ready, being prepared for something, but what.

She would return with me to the States. All my efforts to transfer to South America were an obvious ploy by the Universe to get me to meet her and bring her into my life. We would be married in March of the following year. She became a U.S. citizen three years later. We were in Illinois for several more years before being able to move to Florida.

We had traveled to Colombia on several occasions. She was very protective of me and discouraged me from getting to know the country while there was still guerrilla activities in the rural areas. On our September 2010 trip I persuaded her to allow me to accompany one of her brothers into the country and foothills. I loved what I saw. As we approached a village she told me that her parents would bring the family there during the summer when she was a little girl. The town was famous for its thermal baths.

I took pictures throughout the village then ascended a steep hill in the middle of town where a historic Catholic church had been built. The village was named Usiacuri. After taking pictures of the church I began descending the hill. That's when I heard the voice say,"turn and take a picture of the Sun." I did, and have been ever since. At the same time the title 'Lightstorm' was revealed by the 'Ancients'.

I would take pictures almost daily after returning to our home in Florida.

Chapter 10

Spirit Of El Liberator

On another trip to Colombia we visited 'San Pedro Alejandrino,' in Santa Marta.

Simon Bolivar spent the last days of his life on the estate of a close friend. Now, nearly 200 years later, I walked through the Estancia, slowly, deliberately, soaking in the environment, sensing the Spirit of El Libertador throughout the complex. After some time my step-son signaled me to follow him into another room. Not large, but adequately appointed. Alberto informed me it was the room where the General had passed on.

I had been touched in reading of his leadership and especially his dedication and Love for the people of the Republic that he gave his life to help create. Although he came from a family of wealth his desire was to live free from the Spanish oppression he and all people of the Andes had suffered over the previous 300 years.

Yes, his family had benefited in property and substance as a result of Spanish occupation and he was defined by many by what they saw, not by what he felt in his young years. A fire burned within him for the freeing, liberating, of all people of the Americas. He learned, during his youth, of the organizing of the United States of America and the unveiling of its' Constitution. Bolivar longed for the same in South America. He knew there needed to be a revolution equally as bloody as the one that had taken place further North. He was driven, destined, to be the liberator of this people of the Andes, from the Caribbean in the North all the way to the Southern tip of the continent along the Eastern and Western slopes of the Cordillera.

The battles fought, the blood shed, is all written in the history books. Much of it accurate, some not. What is felt by many to this day is the Spirit of a man destined to lead the common 'peones' and 'campecinos' to victory over Spanish oppression. He helped put South America on a better course. He is as beloved to the American people he liberated in the South as citizens of the United States feel about George Washington in the North.

As I walked into Simon Bolivars sleeping quarters, I stood at the foot of his bed. I closed my eyes and entered into that special place I go when inviting Higher Consciousness to commune with me. I was enveloped in a field of energy that I can only describe as a strong vibration that defined Unconditional Love. It was a particular vibration that I had felt on one other occasion in 1989, in the bedroom at Mount Vernon where George Washington had passed on 190 years earlier, in 1799.

I felt the very same Spirit, Energy. Bolivar's Spirit of dedication to so many millions that had suffered at the hands of ruthless, power hungry individuals, willing to sacrifice the lives of the innocent, whether men, women, or children, to get their way and line their pockets with more riches and power. I could feel the surge of inequality he had felt. That feeling laced with Love for his fellowman encompassed his Soul and lead him through the doors required to pass through to fulfill a divine calling and destiny. It was no wonder I felt the way I did. Bolivar's destiny was equally as important and fulfilling as Washington's.

Bolivar was an enlightened person. A person driven from his youth to help free those he saw abused, exploited and manipulated by the Spanish conquerers.

So, What Has Changed?

Much of the world still remains in bondage, is still abused, exploited and manipulated. It is most obvious in the Middle East as thousands are killed and millions displaced, driven from their homes and towns by the same conquering spirit that ravaged South America. Greedy, egotistical, self appointed aggressors and thugs who have separated themselves from common sense and invented reasons to destroy, claiming justification and exaltation through their god.

All this while power-mongers, hidden in the shadows, aware of the inhumanity through the millennia, lovers of power more than helping advance the Divinity of Consciousness that dwells in all of humanity, continue to choose force over Love, and manipulation more than sharing and offering a hand up. How are these entities any better than those forceful, brutal warriors determined to kill innocence. In this group of cut throats are many of the so called creator gods. The historic treasures of those ancient countries of the Middle East and South America are worth more than their weight in gold. The value of the hearts of the innocent is beyond priceless!

Those in the West who profess freedom are also in a grave dilemma. The mask of materialism is so powerful in blocking Earth energy, hiding the true reason they have incarnated on Earth, that other members of our Cosmic family have offered to assist those who are awakened and others in their awakening. The desire of our Universal family is for all mankind, East as well as West, to have the opportunity to awaken, to experience Consciousness the way it was intended to be experienced.

Liberators are with us today, not involved in the shedding of blood but in the shedding of ignorance, of hopelessness, of abuse, physical, emotional, and psychological, for those who will receive it. Valiant, noble, Souls standing ready to help and support the unfolding of that Divine Source in each individual that chooses to know and embrace their own Higher Consciousness.

The Human Vehicle-A Perfect Creation

I've written throughout this manuscript that the human body is a perfect creation. Within the standard conditioning and manipulation of the human mind this statement is far from true. These bodies we inhabit can seem far from perfect and, in the present conditioning and physical definition of mortality, it is true.

As we awaken to the true meaning of life in a mortal body we begin to allow the divine knowledge of Creation to work in us, to deprogram the worldly knowledge and replace it with the brilliance of Creation in its diversity. To assist us in following our destiny in this mortality.

I have witnessed members of my own family experience the physical, mental, and emotional hardships, of pain and disease causing them, and those around them, much suffering. How they reacted to these experiences is how society and religion has taught them to react. I reacted the same at times, copying them until I realized I didn't feel the remorse, anger, frustration, and finally acceptance of the disease or hardship that they demonstrated. I felt compassion and love for them as they passed through the experience. I had to adjust to my own experiences in the same way. I have learned to respect the journey and embrace the experience. Many times it is difficult, seemingly impossible, but remembering my desire and my plea for higher guidance and enlightenment, these experiences have become a valuable part of the journey. I will not be a victim of this world and its reality.

In March of 1984 I was in Bolivia when I received a telex that my mother had been hospitalized and was on life support. She was 61 years old. I called my father immediately in the hospital where my mother lay dying. He explained what had happened, that the operation was too traumatic for her body to accept. If she didn't respond by the following day he would act on her previous wishes and have her removed from life support. Her body was still alive. The thought of catching a flight to be at her side before she passed entered my mind but was immediately enveloped by my mothers own message,"I am fine. You are where God wants you at this moment. Don't worry about me, don't feel guilt in any sense." I didn't. I remained in La Paz for another two days before returning to Kemmerer, Wyoming for her funeral. I never felt a need to grieve at her death. She wasn't dead. I celebrated in my heart since I knew she had completed her mission in that perfect body. I never felt a separation. I felt joy because she was still with me. She always will be.

The body is created according to our needs as we accept a new incarnation. We have input in the creation and preparation of the body by and through our parents. It is prepared so it can introduce us to the experiences we want or need throughout the destined course of our physical existence. We also programmed much of our relationships in each specific lifetime, especially intimate relationships. Even specific illnesses and events had been programmed as well as how they would affect us and those around us. These creations teach us. How shall we learn if there is no vehicle to enter? That vehicle is created to perfectly match the challenges we need during our lifetime.

Valiant Souls

There have been valiant Souls throughout history that have freed the downtrodden, like Simon Bolivar and George Washington, then there have been those noble Souls who have silently led the fight against this world without receiving accolades and worldly honors, like a mother protecting and teaching her child, a father giving respect and direction, even reaching through the dimensions to counsel and advise after passing through. Love is immortal, interdimensional.

As we learn this valuable lesson through Higher Consciousness we can help and support one another in this wonderful journey. True happiness and joy comes as a result of our understanding the journey, this incarnation in this vehicle, this body, this perfect creation.

Chapter 11

My Mentors

Being religious and being spiritual are not the same. Being spiritual does not require religion. Many ecclesiastical leaders claim that being religious is being spiritual. Thinking of a God as taught by religions of the world can invoke feelings of a loving father figure on one hand and as a jealous vindictive one on the other. An all powerful being who can reward us to heaven or condemn us to hell.

I observed in my parents a great respect for others. We would visit Indian festivals around the Pacific Northwest on a regular basis. While I saw others, at a young age, belittle the indigenous tribal communities around Spokane my parents spoke of their history and love of Mother Earth. My father had learned from them as a boy growing up in the Wind River Mountains in Wyoming. He became so good at catching trophy size brown and brook trout out of the streams around the ranch where he lived that he was sought out by many well-to-do fly fishermen from California to show them where and how to catch the 'big ones'. His talent was in his patience to watch the habits and movements of the native wildlife then design a system to catch them. The same as the indigenous tribes had done for millennia. He was not shy about his respect for these people. He carried that respect over in his everyday dealings with all people. My mother taught us likewise, to do good to others, always.

My parents laid a good foundation, however, at times I showed less respect for myself than for others. I believe it is a human reaction based on our religious training and upbringing. Although I have not been haunted by that feeling for many years now, I still see it daily in those around me. It becomes very easy to insert some positive words of respect and Love when I have the opportunity to speak with them.

Kindness and compassion can and should be a part of everyones life, whether religious or not. The question we should be asking ourselves is not which God or belief system to follow, but am I true to myself. Am I getting out of life what I came here for or am I pushing my way through just to get what I want? Am I getting joy out of life, am I doing good to others? Am I sharing? Am I Compassionate?

Who has affected the most change for good in your life? As children, we look up to those around us, especially our parents. We expect to get ideas, direction, and counsel from them as well as others we are surrounded with as we mature.

As a four year old I looked up to my brother, ten years old and so mature. I tried to copy his example. He was quite rebellious and independent. I was the third in line and somewhat more mellow. When I attempted to mimic his actions I couldn't garner the same results. When he stretched the limits of his bounds Mom would attempt to punish him. He would turn and laugh in her face, then that famous sentence,"You just wait till your father gets home."

I thought, "If he can do it, I can too."

The next time I found myself in trouble, I remembered my brothers example. I would do the same. My mothers words, even when they were meant to chastise and get my attention, were words of love and it brought tears to my eyes. I knew I had done wrong and learned from her stern, yet loving, demeanor. I didn't have to wait till my father got home.

While my brother was several years older than me, I continued to learn from his actions throughout my life, as I still do now even though he has passed on. He could show a good heart but it was used mainly to advance his own agenda and to influence positive opinions toward himself, a common flaw in worldly man. He did some good things for others but only if it was beneficial to him.

He was very intelligent and a tremendous researcher of Mormon history. On some occasions he confided in me that some of the church doctrine was flawed. An obvious one was the Law of Polygamy, he suggested to me that it was more sexually oriented than inspired of God, yet in the same breath he mentioned that when Joseph Smiths' body was disinterred some time after his death, his body was still there, he did not leave any trace of a resurrection. He believed Smith to be of such a stature in life that he would, like Jesus, be resurrected upon death. When he did the research on the disinterment explaining the state of Smiths' remains, he told me he felt that the resurrection may only affect the DNA not the actual flesh of the individual. I thought, "there's much more to it than that." As humans we tend to believe what we convince ourselves of, even when the evidence is to the contrary.

I didn't want to get into a deep discussion with him. I learned to keep my thoughts to myself. I had learned on more than one occasion that if I shared some personal inspiration with him, even if he felt the legitimacy of it, it would be rejected only to surface several days later in one of his lectures declaring it as his own idea or inspiration. Words would come into my heart encouraging me to be careful where I cast my pearls.

I loved my brother but more so from a distance. He was more interested in his fame within ecclesiastical circles in the hierarchy of the church and I believed he was in good company. He always felt a need to mentor me, being his younger brother, yet I found him swallowed up in his own ambition and often jealous of my accomplishments in giving my time and talents to people in need of compassion and support throughout the third world countries I worked in.

The Samoan, Fijian, Bolivian, and African people I served were wonderful mentors and will always remain so in my heart.

I reflected, on some occasions, about the relationship my father and I had. I felt my father showed the same amount of love for my brother as he did for me. I loved him for the non-prejudicial way he approached all people. He would expound the importance of treating women with great respect. The Love he had for my grandmother, though having passed on many years before, he also showed for my mother. There was always a strong presence of respect and Love, and he showed me by example.

My mother, likewise, showed great respect, dedication, and Love for my father. She sustained him in his business, his church responsibilities, and most of all in the home. When one or more of the seven children needed disciplining, they would back each other so we never witnessed them arguing over one being right and the other wrong. Consistency.

When I was thirteen and learning to flex my likes and dislikes, I became lax on one of my chores. Both Mom and Dad had asked me to follow through with the chore. In my laziness I failed. Dad came home from work. He noticed that I had done nothing. I was sitting in the living room watching television. I heard his gruff voice as he opened the door coming from the garage. I thought I knew what was coming. I jumped up from the chair and headed out the front door, with Dad right on my heals. As I made a left turn around to the back of the house, I began to pull away from him. I was faster than him now. He couldn't catch me. Thoughts were rushing through my head. What do I do now? I'll have to stop sometime! This is the only home I know!

I stopped in my tracks, turned to face him, and take my punishment. He looked in to my eyes and said, "Son, will you please take care of your responsibilities?"

"Yes, Dad," I said. There was no more discussion. From then on I took care of my chores, religiously.

Wind River Man

I had such reverence for my father and his Love for me throughout my life. I knew he was fallible, like other people, yet I also knew he had a tender and loving heart and wished only the best for this Earth and all of creation.

He loved music and played his guitar and sang songs to us, his children, that he had learned while living and working on the ranch in the Wind River Mountains of Wyoming as a young boy and man.

At fourteen years of age while living in Uruguay, I informed my father of my desire to learn to play the guitar. A friend lent me his guitar while my father taught me basic chords. I was hooked and the music became an outlet for me throughout my entire life. My father saw my dedication and gifted me with a beautiful Brazilian guitar of my own. It quickly became my most precious possession.

I began putting together lyrics of my own to accompany the music I was learning to play on the guitar. Ten years passed and I completed my required missionary duty for the church and college education and I was living in Missouri. I formed a band that performed around the Kansas City area for a short time. Though we de-solved the group I continued writing my music.

In the previous years I had been almost haunted by the stories my father had told me of the Wind Rivers and his childhood without a father to guide him. The words kept flowing into my heart, "Wind River Man the mountains whisper out your name." I knew there would be more lyrics coming to complete the song, with time.

As I tapped into Higher Consciousness, without really understanding that I was doing so, I began to form the feelings and words for my fathers journey. The lyrics to "Wind River Man" took form in my heart, my mind and then to script.

Wind River Man

by Robert F Allen

A boy goes through his childhood
And learns to be a man
With no father there to teach him
Still, he learns the best he can

A summer storm calls to him
To the Mountains he will roam
A boy sets out to learn about
The Mountains he calls home

As time goes by on Mountains high
A seed is planted here

In the young boys heart he learns his part
'neath heavens bright and clear

Wind River Man the Mountains
whisper out your name
In the Summer breeze or Winter freeze
Their song is still the same

The young boy grows, the Mountains know
That he must leave some day
With wisdom learned a young man yearns
To go along his way

Far away from Mountains beautiful
Now, with children of his own
He teaches them how it had been
On the Mountains he called home

Wind River Man the Mountains
whisper out your name
In the Summer breeze or Winter freeze
Their song is still the same

Through the softness of his smile
My father tells these tales to me

Of Mountains high and beautiful
Of Gods creatures roaming, living to be free

Wind River Man the Mountains
whisper out your name
In the Summer breeze or Winter freeze
Their song is still the same

~O~

My fathers influence on me is strong to this day.
Where he found joy in his life, he sought to share
it with his siblings, at times forceful, as well as with
his children. He did it out of the greatest Love
within his heart. He desired all people to feel the
joy that came to him from his church.

The last years of his life were confusing since
he could not separate his love for his God and
Savior from the church. Since passing on, my
father experienced the Mormon community on
the other side. He received answers there from
Guides and Messengers that could not get
through to him while in this dimension. Thirteen
years after his passing he came to me, and others
around me, to ask me to forgive him and to let me

know that he understood why I had to do what I did. He went on to explain that he would be with me and support me in my endeavor to help in the Awakening.

When I Was a Little Boy

My Mother passed in 1984, thirteen years before my father, eight years before I left the church. She was not as dedicated to religion as my father but remained quiet about her feelings. A year before she passed on she made a trip to visit her youngest sister, a Baptist, who never supported anything about Mormonism. Mom talked to her openly about the problems and the sacrifices she and Dad had experienced while working overseas. She then proceeded to talk about her concern for me. She said she had been worried about my future, spiritually not physically. She knew of my lack of dedication to the family religion. My Aunt told her that she was much more concerned about my brothers spiritual future than mine. She assured my mother that I would find my way.

My Mother was a wonderful inspiration to do what is right and honorable throughout life. She has been very active in my life since 1984. I have spoken to her many times and she lets me know when she's near. I have photographed her on several occasions. She is a Noble Creation.

I learned to play a ballad on my guitar about Mothers. I taught my children the same song. It clearly explains my relationship with her.

When I Was a Little Boy
by Mike Settle

When I was a little boy, my mother said to me, "Watch the new born roses grow. It's a pretty sight to see.

You, my son, shall blossom as the flower below. I will be your raindrops. You will be my rose.

Listen while I tell you of the beauty in the sky. There's a home for angels on the clouds so high.

Many times I wonder on the clouds above is it my dear mother who showers me with love?

We all have mentors in our lives. They teach us by example more than words, by showing patience when we make mistakes, knowingly or unknowingly. They come from all walks of life and many times don't even realize they are mentoring us. We are all teachers and students. I may be in the minority having had parents who were so effective in teaching, leading, and stepping aside to allow me to fulfill my walk in this life. I have been Blessed.

Chapter 12

Other Messengers

Universal Consciousness has always existed. There is nothing new about some of the information in this book. This information, however, will be new to many. As you begin to study, meditate and seek understanding you will begin to notice little things you have previously overlooked because your focus was on getting ahead in this world.

Life takes on new meaning, in fact the true definition of life comes into focus as the world consciousness takes a back seat. You may not have all the answers to life's questions at once, but you are learning how to access the knowledge that has always been there. You will be directed to information available in writings by authors that have experienced this Universal Consciousness and are expanding their experience and knowledge by sharing it with humankind.

One of these 'messengers' of Light and Knowledge is Brian L. Weiss M.D. The following is an excerpt from one of his international bestsellers, "Many Lives, Many Masters."

In a deep hypnotic state, his patient Catherine explains what she sees, as Dr. Weiss asks,

"Are you resting?"

"Yes ... jewels of different colors ... ."

"Jewels?"

"Yes. They're really lights, but they look like jewels ... ."

"What else?" I asked.

"I just . . ." she paused, and then her whisper was loud and firm. "There are many words and thoughts that are flying around. . . . It's about coexistence and harmony . . . the balance of things." I knew the Masters were nearby.

"Yes," I urged her on. "I want to know about these things. Can you tell me?"

"Right now they're just words," she answered.

"Coexistence and harmony," I reminded her. When she answered, it was the voice of the poet master. I was thrilled to hear from him again.

"Yes," he answered. "Everything must be balanced. Nature is balanced. The beasts live in harmony. Humans have not learned to do that. They continue to destroy themselves. There is no harmony, no plan to what they do. It's so different in nature. Nature is balanced. Nature is energy and life . . . and restoration. And humans just destroy. They destroy nature. They destroy other humans. They will eventually destroy themselves."

This was an ominous prediction. With the world constantly in chaos and turmoil I hoped this would not be soon. "When will this happen?" I asked.

"It will happen sooner than they think. Nature will survive. Plants will survive. But we will not."

"Can we do anything to prevent that destruction?"

"No. Everything must be balanced. . . ."

"Will this destruction happen in our lifetime? Can we avert it?"

"It will not happen in our lifetime. We will be on another plane. Another dimension, when it happens, but we will see it."

"Is there no way of teaching humankind?" I kept looking for a way out, for some mitigating possibility.

"It will be done on another level. We will learn from that."

I looked on the bright side. "Well, then our souls progress in different places." Awakened man becomes Awakened Man.

"Yes. We will no longer be . . . here, as we know it. We will see it."

"Yes," I conceded. "I have a need to reach these people, but I don't know how to reach them. Is there a way, or do they have to learn this for themselves?"

"You cannot reach everyone. In order to stop the destruction you must reach everyone, and you cannot. It cannot be stopped. They will learn. When they progress, they will learn. There will be peace, but not here, not here in this dimension."

"Eventually, there will be peace?"

"Yes, on another level."

"It seems so far away, though," I complained. "People seem so petty now . . . greedy, power hungry, ambitious. They forget about love and understanding and knowledge. There is so much to learn."

"Yes."

"Can I write anything to help these people? Is there a way?"

"You know the way. We do not have to tell you. It will all be to no avail, for we will all reach the level, and they will see. We are all the same. One is no greater than the next. And all this is just lessons and . . . punishment (pages 158-159).

The Nature Of Mankind

In these vehicles we call bodies, exists the Soul. For my own benefit I call it Consciousness. It is linked to the Divine, and in fact is Divine. Consciousness is God and the portion of Consciousness that inhabits my body has learned some very fascinating things.

Once I've learned and observed my body as a vehicle to teach me, my life has taken on a different view of humanity, the Cosmos, the Universe, and Infinity. It has caused me to soar in my thoughts and actions yet at times has caused me to envelope myself in disgust for the actions of ruthless governments, societies, cultures, religions as well as individuals bent on power through deception with the pure intent to control as many as possible and acquire as many possessions as possible. At times I found it difficult to hold back my words and would say something that wouldn't be translatable to a solely three dimensional mind, yet I've seen the light in them shift to seek understanding in the comment, Sowing.

Even though the world is caught up in power, possessions, and ego, the Divine within them can be penetrated and awakened through proper intent. The choice is theirs even though the words or events come from outside their vehicle.

The common, unenlightened person in the world has no concept of life outside himself other than what he can see with his own eyes, what he can hear with his own ears, and what he can touch. At times he can't even believe that. It can be too incredible to accept so he blanks it out of his senses.

Just the opposite is the case. Life exists everywhere. Nothing exists that is not Light. Even the dark matter that is being discussed by the scientific world as to what it is, is Light, Light in its purest form. Light is infinite with infinite frequencies and moves freely within its own existence to experience infinite realities. It experiences my own existence in this physical body, the highs and lows, the joys and sorrows, the sweetness and bitterness that I have experienced while in this dimension. All actions and events are recorded in the Universe, in Light.

Within our Consciousness exists the ability to access all knowledge and information even while in these bodies. All that is required is the knowledge and intent to unlock these mortal vehicles to allow us to experience the Universe in a way that cannot be experienced without the body. A fascinating thought!

"The Ancients" have instructed me throughout my lifetime. As they became more obvious to me they openly identified themselves. From that time I was able to recall the subtle messages and nudges they had given me along the way. I began to understand my existence before this lifetime and the relationships I had established over the eons of time and how they have come to assist me in my direction and destiny in this lifetime. I knew I was never alone!

History has shown us the attributes of mankind. In general, man is aggressive, greedy, and power hungry. There have been exceptions. There have been examples set by the Masters, the Messengers throughout history. We have had the key that unlocks the door to this understanding as long as humankind has lived on Earth.

There have been those that have declared themselves Masters who are not. They have been sent to deceive, to persuade through eloquent words and declare miracles when there were none. These intruders have convinced many along the way, even entire cultures. Borders have been established. Wars have been declared and fought, and even to this very day the bloodshed, the threats, the declarations of wickedness in the name of their god or gods are witnessed by all on the evening world news.

This world will, indeed, feel the consequences of its actions. As I mentioned earlier, the Earth is even now, recompensing man for its misuse. Nature will survive. Man, in his present state will not. Religion will not. Those who seek truth at all cost, follow it and learn to ascend in their thoughts and actions, will literally be transformed to the higher dimension. This is not the resurrection preached of in religions throughout the world. Ascension will take place as the individual learns how to ascend.

It has been the nature of people in religious positions of power and authority throughout history to declare doctrines, sacred teachings and even visions, as revelations directly from God. The masses have, in many cases, been willing to accept them as such when they were nothing more than whims and inventions of men and creator gods in powerful positions cementing in the masses a need to keep the power hungry leaders in their 'sacred and holy calling.'

There have, however, been women and men throughout history, placed here to be Messenger Guides to those who would listen. In many cases the message was so powerful and inspiring that the multitudes could not ignore them. Scribes throughout history have also credited these Messenger Guides with teachings they did not profess. These modified teachings were incorporated into much of what Christianity is today. It is called 'twisting the truth' and using bits of their teachings to deceive the masses. It is a practice that has been quite effective throughout time.

If one pursues the teachings of Jesus, for example, to the earliest record, one will find Holy men and women, different from what the Bible claimed, teaching truths that were in line with what one discovers when accessing Universal Consciousness. They never issued commandments. They never preached doctrines. They taught people to Love one another. They taught by example. John, who is called the Baptist, was one of these teachers. At the time of these Master Teachers there were those who wanted to, and did, declare John as their Messiah. John declared he was not their Messiah, that there would be no Messiah. Guides and Messengers would deliver truths to move the individual to awaken to their own majesty, their own divinity, no one individual being greater than another. He and others taught of Ascension and nothing of resurrection. Ascension is attained by the individual. There was never a need for a Savior or Messiah.

Resurrection had been believed and taught in cultures dating back as far as 3000 B.C. The same with the Immaculate Conception and virgin birth. These legends and myths were never based in Consciousness. There have been those Master Teachers and Messengers who have taught of Ascension through knowledge, wisdom and Love. It was never a gift, as the teaching of the resurrection is, and was created and taught by command throughout Christianity by those inventors of the doctrine.

The knowledge of Ascension is more obtainable today than it has ever been. There is no Second Coming of Jesus because there was no resurrection in the first place. Ascension, on the other hand, can take place any time the individual is ready. If one is not prepared, then death, as the world knows it, takes place. Those who have any understanding of the Creator realize there is no death. There are transitions from one life to the next, one dimension to the next. The Soul never dies. We are not the bodies we inhabit. We are merely experiencing emotions that cannot be experienced in any other way. We are Light experiencing physical joy, pain, happiness, sadness . . . all emotions.

Some of the other messengers throughout this current 'cycle of civilization' are known to us through the Torah. Enoch Ascended. Moses Ascended. Elijah Ascended. Others Ascended that are not in any record we currently have.

Today we have a world of information, through the Internet, at our fingertips. It is a wonderful tool to have available. Yet this tool is misused. It is meant to bring the world closer together. For the most part it is not. The world is more set on getting ahead. Of having more wealth and riches. Of being 'one up' on the next guy.

There are Messengers that can be accessed at any time using the Internet. There are wonderful books available. The journey begins with you. Seek and you shall find! Go within. Meditate. Call on your Higher Self. Your Higher Self will never deceive you.

Deprogramming The Internal Computer

Our physical vehicle is a computer. There has been a lifetime of programing to condition us to this world. It's time to de-program, uninstall. You can learn to discard the dross and use the good. Invite the higher vibrations, where Truth is eternal, to come into you and change your life. You already know what knowledge and Truth within you should remain. Not all programming mankind has received has been bad. It's through accessing your Higher Self that you become aware what truths have been intertwined with deceptive teachings and conditioning.

As this process of deprogramming continues you will notice more than subtle changes in your demeanor. I went through several layers of emotions, feelings I didn't realize were there.

I recall a very emotional event I experienced as I realized I had to erase all the religious training and conditioning if I was intent on going forward.

I didn't hesitate. I was still willing to pay the price for Enlightenment, Truth.

I pictured myself in a spacious classroom. The walls were covered with chalkboards three tiers high. On them were written all the important teachings of my lifetime to that date. Teachings of my parents, of my peers, of grade school, high school and University teachers and professors. Some teachings shared out of Love, along with lessons I was demanded to learn from school and university and especially from religion. I saw a chord of fear woven throughout all lessons transcribed on the chalkboards. All of the teachings, even those taught out of Love, insisted in the realization of these teachings, over the period of my lifetime would bring, in some cases, financial rewards, accolades, possibly even honors. In others the possibility of reaching the highest kingdom of glory in heaven through the grace of someone exalted, after doing all I could for myself.

Visualizing all of this history of my learning, in one swift mental act, one of defiance to this world, I erased all that the chalkboards contained.

The entire mental image of my learning over the previous 45 years to that moment was erased.

The chalkboards were empty, bare of all the teachings I had allowed in my life. Teachings I had allowed due to my culture, my family, and the religion I was born in to.

What would happen now? I stood firm in my desire to know what really had caused the world to be in such a state of fear.

I blurted out in a loud voice, "Now! I want you to teach me! I want to know all!"

I didn't even know who I was talking to. It certainly wasn't the God of religion(s). I directed my hearts desires to something or someone much more exalted than anything religion could imagine.

Had I made the right decision? YES!

A Transformation

I would begin to increase in understanding. I would have instantaneous responses to my queries. All answers came from within myself. Some things were already known as I drew them out of Consciousness. Others were shown to Consciousness, to further Enlighten my vehicle (physical body/mind), by Messengers called 'The Ancients'. They spoke to me many times over the years, in fact, I would come to know that they had been involved in my teaching throughout my life.

Erasing the chalkboards did not erase the goodness I retained in my heart and Soul. 'The Ancients' are constant in my life. A few years ago they appeared to me. The first thing they said was, "We are many but we speak with one voice".

I was able to ask them a specific question.

"Am I one of You?" I said.

"No," they answered. "You are from beyond."

I needed not ask more. I will be shown more in the future when it is time. They showed me Light and Spirit beyond description, then the scene closed as they departed.

We attract what we need, to learn. We attract those who can teach us, those in our everyday life and those in our interdimensional life.

Being Bold!

Prior to an awakening to our Divine self we have all felt alone. One of the many ploys of mortality showered upon us from creator gods. As the body recognizes its place to teach Consciousness, as well as learn from it, the awakening takes place. Imagine our Earth filled with awakened humanity. What will we have accomplished? We would all work in harmony with one another, the family unit would be much different. No fear of intimidation from angry, frustrated people, only support and Love confronting and meeting challenges to assist us and others in our growth through Divinity into higher dimensions.

To those aware of Consciousness in them, this process has already begun. Our direction is to sow goodness along the way and confront the world attitude with great force knowing we are supported by our Awakened Family here and throughout frequency and dimensions. Stand up to the world with all strength of force. Say what comes to your lips to counter the intimidation and fear behind the worlds attacks. Put people of the world in their place. Speak words that prick their souls, penetrate into their Consciousness and move them toward Awakening.

This is not the time nor place to be timid. It is time to take our place in this historic movement to Awakening the planet, reclaiming our connection with Earth as she also ascends in Her Awakening.

Much of the western world feels it can be repaired through modifying the present system of capitalism. Putting hope in the next wave of politicians promising to save us in our ignorance by bettering the already broken, perverted economic program that has proven time and again it is fallible. It protects the unjust money mongers and penalizes the honorable lower classes, classes that do not exist in a higher frequency of Consciousness. The economic system now ruling the world would not exist in a society where Divinity is known, Consciousness is understood and the physical vehicle is allowed to ascend to higher dimensions.

We should and would be allowed to freely express ideas, inspirations and inventions with anyone. Sharing suggestions, ideas and concepts that would benefit all of humanity with the remuneration being the further uplifting and advancement of all Earth dwellers, moving us all toward one higher dimension after another, infinitely!

We have seen the beautiful photography given to us by the many telescopes sent into space. All the information recorded in the many photos can never be totally deciphered in this three dimensional reality. Many times we don't even understand what we are looking at, so science and math take over in an attempt to translate and decipher the recorded information. The only hope the scientific world has is in working with higher Consciousness to then gain the wisdom behind the information. An interesting thought to then pose is whether science continues in its quest upon learning about the higher dimensions or will have all queries been answered satisfying the appetite of those in the lower third dimension?

Awakening to higher Consciousness gives the individual access to all information and wisdom. Not that all is immediately known but the key has been earned and unlocked the door to the Universe and the individual then enters and progresses at his or her own pace.

'As a man thinks so shall he become.' Evidence of this ancient Irish saying is seen in every person that has ever lived upon the Earth. We are what we think. We become what we believe. We are fed information and dogma from our infancy and we believe it, then put it into action throughout our lives until something causes us to change our thinking. It may be a different dogma or belief. People change religions, political beliefs, even sexual orientation as their opinions change. This is part of the human experience.

The Awakening is different. Information received in the Awakening process does not come from any outside source. It is information already in your Consciousness and is activated by you. You don't have to decide whether it's true or not. Truth is experienced throughout your physical body translated through Consciousness. As we Awaken we reflect on decisions and choices we made throughout our lives. Some may have brought good results to us and our surroundings, others may not have produced the good outcome we had intended. We now reflect on the past experiences of our life and review the results through our Awakening. What is interesting to discover is that all we have experienced has brought us to this point in our never ending path of learning and progressing toward higher dimension. What we may have thought or been taught was a sin, or sinful, then becomes the learning experience, and guilt, as prescribed by the world becomes null and void. Guilt is replaced by knowledge and experience through higher Consciousness.

Everything we experience through mortality is a stepping stone to assist in our desire to ascend to higher dimensions. As we awaken to Consciousness within these bodies we learn the true value these physical creations are and can continue perfecting them as we go. If we choose, there can come a time when we do not have to leave our bodies in what the world calls death.

We can continue to perfect them as our body ascends with us.

Consciousness is Supreme Creator. Consciousness is Source. Awakened man becomes Awakened Man. All gods and creators are self appointed, less than Awakened Man. Awakened Man is Supreme Creator. Through Awakened Man we arrive at the Fountain of Consciousness.

We Are The Designers of Our Journey

We prepare our own life story prior to our birth, before each lifetime. We all have relationships that have been established over the eons of time. We all have experienced many intimate relationships through many lifetimes and intermediate lifetimes. We can meet several different companions in or during one lifetime. Some times we experience only one.

At times, as in my case, we can be introduced to a companion during the dream stage of sleep. I was eighteen and it was not a dream, it was very real, inter-dimensional. Sexual relationships do exist inter-dimensionally. I kept it to myself because it could not be explained within my religion. One of the overpowering feelings I had during the experience was that we knew each other over the eons of time. I could describe her features, her touch, her smell.

I wouldn't meet her, physically, for another twenty-six years. We would have the relationship confirmed and blessed by the 'Ancients', then progress to other relationships, separately, feeling no guilt, only acceptance of the connection and a desire to continue in the physical experience with Consciousness.

Rituals, Ceremonies, and Secret Signs

It becomes important to explain about rituals, ceremonies, and secret signs that have been interjected and allowed to evolve throughout our present 'cycle of civilization'. I mentioned previously that the commandments that we have been indoctrinated with throughout the past three and one half millennia did not come from Source. They came from creator gods and their ambassadors here in this dimension. Supreme Creator has never issued commandments to humankind. If that were the case then free-will would have been circumvented.

The same situation includes rituals, rights, secret ceremonies, and secret signs. None have been ordained by Supreme Creator, Source, the Fountain of Truth and Knowledge, Consciousness.

The pomp and ceremony is all associated with the importance and glamour that is religion. It is meant to cement the relationship that one acquires with a particular church or organization along the way during this lifetime.

As a young man, I accepted secret endowments of a so called 'higher dispensation' through temple rituals. I was taught by my parents that it was the godly thing to do. Along with completing those secret/sacred ceremonies I was required to dawn 'temple undergarments', reminding me of the endowments I had taken upon myself. There were special markings strategically placed on the garment. The specific shape of these markings was very much like those of another order outside of that religion. I was intimidated by the statement in the ceremonies that if I revealed any part of this ritual I would 'suffer my life to be taken'. That was many years ago and perhaps the religion has changed its dialog to exclude that now, however, I have never forgotten those words and I celebrated the day I shed those garments for good. It was the last physical act of defiance I showed to the church and its creator gods as I exited that reality.

Keeping rituals 'secret' because they are 'sacred' has nothing to do with Source. It is the product of lower thinking within this third dimension. Nothing is secret to those who truly seek. Source hides nothing.

Upon my final physical act of leaving the reality of religion I was blessed with a clearer vista and understanding of my direction and destiny.

This m.o. has been around for thousands of years. It's recorded in Sumerian history and especially on the walls of the temples and tombs of Egypt. Much of what has happened in the past has repeated itself over and over.

A Modern Day Exodus

The events that led up to the deliverance of a generation of people three thousand five hundred years ago is repeating itself today. This is not a religious event. Neither was the deliverance at the time of Moses. Historians turned it into a religious event. It was not!! Neither is the one occurring today. Religion is not invited! An open heart and a desire to understand Consciousness are the only prerequisites. That comes from intent within each individual.

This gathering of Consciousness is without borders. It embraces the goodness found in each heart, in each life directed towards the Divine. This revolution through Consciousness will succeed because it will be done from within not from outside powers and organizations. Our assistance comes from the Cosmos, from our future where we are already victorious. Consciousness is not on a timetable. It exists in all dimensions and space. All is present. There is no past nor future, only the now.

All countries belong to humanity, and humanity belongs to the Earth. The American dream is more than a dream and a goal for those who reside there. The pursuit of freedom and happiness knows no boundary. America and the Spirit of America does not belong to the government nor any religion. It belongs to the people of the Earth. The pursuit of how one worships has nothing to do with freedoms, in fact, it is possibly the greatest deterrent to an individuals freedom and personal growth. Worship does not exist in Consciousness. We are not required to worship ourselves nor others.

The time has come for governments to relinquish their hold on humanity. They are to serve us not control us. We are asserting our desires and actions to assist in this change. The spread of compassion and understanding of Consciousness and the Ascension to higher vibrations and dimensions will not be subverted. No shedding of innocent blood will take place by being involved in this revolution. Those determined to continue on in the control of the world through their perverted zealot beliefs will be herded and controlled by intradimensional entities from areas in the Middle East where they will continue the worship of their false gods through bloodshed until they discover they have been manipulated by those charlatans concealed in frequency above and beneath the Earth. The roundup will not be only for fundamentalist Muslims, it will include fundamentalists from every corner of the Earth who only accept the eradication of those opposed to their form of worship and belief, Christianity included.

The Wall

See yourself standing upon the Earth. The environment is breathtaking and inviting to the Soul. The Earth and the Cosmos are feeding you with information about Creation, about humanity, about the future of mankind. What will be achieved, not what can be achieved.

As you observe from a distance, you see yourself increasing in Light and understanding of the Eternal purpose of Life, of Consciousness. You reflect upon your birth, then conditioning by your parents, other family members and friends, church and society. As you do, a circular Wall appears around you growing higher and higher blocking the beautiful vistas you saw before the Wall appeared.

The Wall becomes so prevalent in your life that others define who you are by it. You yourself are convinced that the Wall is a reflection of who and what you are. As you turn around you see only Wall, and then upon it, scenes appear and it becomes a literal 'theatre in the round' showing your life up to that point-in-time. Then scenes of your future, based upon your conditioning, appear. Sacrifice and hope that your good works will save you are among the most consistent teachings you are brainwashed with. The Wall grows higher and higher, the scenes become increasingly more insistent that you must surrender to your conditioning and brainwashing.

You may have become very wealthy and successful in the worlds' eyes, and the world demands all the credit, and you are to teach others that what you accomplished is due to your 'conditioning'. That if everyone followed your example they too would become wealthy.

On the other hand you may be living in dire poverty. In society's eyes you have failed. You have not followed the conditioning you were told was necessary to survive in this world. You become a lesson for those along the way that are pushing for financial success and acceptance in society.

"See what can happen to you if you do not follow the worlds teachings and demand for obedience!" The Wall is a teacher. A teacher of 'reality', but only the reality within the circular wall!

Something within you speaks to your heart and declares, "this is not what I was created for. I am focusing on something that was not there in the beginning!"

Consciousness is reminding you of the breathtaking scenes and the beauty of your creation. It is reminding you that the Wall is just that. Walls can be torn down. You must not be afraid to 'look up', then 'look down.' Above you are the Cosmos, beneath your feet is the Earth. They both are constant. There is no false reality here. There is only Love. Love manifest in information, in the understanding of all things, in Light.

As you continue viewing yourself within this circular wall, you watch as your eyes turn toward the Cosmos, then to the Earth beneath. You are remembering with your Heart, your Soul. Light appears, flowing into your being from above. More light appears ascending from the Earth beneath.

The light merges in your soul. You awaken, then you remember that this has always been so. The Light has and will always be flowing into, and through you.

You witness the Wall shrinking, getting smaller and smaller. It disappears, but the teachings, the control through conditioning remains in your memory and now becomes a tool against itself as you share your awakening with others.

You recall that the greater teachings remembered are those you received from your experiences, especially your failures and the more humble of people along the way, perhaps even the beggar and the homeless. In many instances they are the richest among us.

When you overcome your fears you attract others to yourself and recognize Interdimensional Guides and Messengers that have been with you all along. You have become a Teacher and Messenger of Light yourself. You are Ascending.

Chapter 13

Spirit

Spirit is Energy, and Energy is Light. It is infinite and exists on all levels, in all frequencies and dimensions. Those of lower frequencies can transmit misleading or even harmful messages, usually to people with limited mediumistic ability or lack of spiritual development. Spirits of higher levels seem to be accessible only to those people with higher spiritual development or those with proper intent, those without ulterior motives for self gain or at the expense of others.

"When you meet a seer or wise teacher whose motive is to help others to understand, to heal other people's hearts and to assist them on their spiritual path, a profound shift in your Consciousness can occur. The world will seem different, filled with unseen helpers and bathed in a loving energy that refreshes and renews your soul." <u>Messages from the Masters</u>, Brian Weiss M.D.(pg. 187)

History is filled with legends of visitors from other dimensions and worlds. From the Sumerians and the Messengers from above, to the Maya and Quetzalcoatl, to the Zuni and the Star people. Abraham, Moses, Elijah and Ezekiel in the Torah spoke of contact with 'higher intelligence.' Countless stories of visions of Mary, even God the Father, Jesus, and all the major prophets of the Bible appearing to deliver messages of hope or devastation. Many predicting the end of the world on a specific day or at a specific time.

While contact certainly has been made at different times throughout history, not all contact has been from benevolent sources. Others have, throughout history, claimed revelation from

God when introducing and canonizing doctrine accredited to God when it was purely the doctrine of men, or through creator gods, set in place to manipulate and control the masses through fear.

Some self proclaimed Christian churches are nothing more than cults claiming superior knowledge and revelation as a result of open visions of ancient prophets endowing this 'end time' generation with all the authority necessary to declare devastation to all those who do not accept their 'prophets' as 'mouthpieces' of God on Earth and embrace their faith. This also is nothing more than an attempt to control through fear and manipulation.

The True Messenger

The true Messengers have never led nor taught through fear. They were and are examples of Love. They always understood that the greatest leaders of humankind have always been the greatest of servants. They have always taught that we are all connected to Source. We are all part of the One, having come to this earth to experience emotion, of which Love is the greatest. We have also come here to exercise free-will.

When we talk of Spirit or spiritual things, it envisions in the mind religious teachings, or at the very least belief in a God. Many I speak to today realize that a belief in God has nothing to do with religion. Many are breaking away from religion because of the control it exercises over mankind. The desire to know truth, and actively pursue it, is growing. Many previously religious people are not openly accepting or blindly believing what is preached from the pulpit. Alleluia!

There are those that understand that religion extends beyond the pulpit. Religion is also a cause, principle, or activity pursued with zeal or conscientious devotion. Religion, then, takes on a greater role in our daily lives as we allow it.

Where do you direct your passion?

What Is Passion?

The dictionary defines passion as a powerful emotion, such as love, joy, hatred or anger. Ardent love. Strong sexual desire; lust. The object of such love or desire. Boundless enthusiasm.

The most powerful emotion we can amplify through the human experience is Love. Experienced within Love is the need to be free. The problem mankind has created and continues to promulgate is looking outwardly for a deliverer, someone to step up and free them from bondage. The deliverer is within each individual. When the freedom to express with passion is driven by Love there is no hatred nor anger or fear. Hatred cannot control Love and Love strives to control nothing. Love is. Religion has notoriously indoctrinated its congregations through fear. The teachings of a jealous God, of hell, of satan, of the Bible being the irrevocable, indisputable word of God. These teachings were put in place to control and manipulate humankind.

A born-again Christian, or a passionate Christian by any definition, will state that their religion does not control them. They believe in God because they have faith in Him. That He lives and that they will live with Him in heaven one day.

Religious faith then is not knowing but believing in something or someone. "I hope I'm worthy enough to go to heaven. I don't want to go to hell!" A common statement throughout Christianity.

The religion of my parents teaches that one should seek truth and that all truth is, or will be, embraced by the church. It also teaches that only the head of the church has direct access to God and whatever 'revelation' he receives from God is to be believed without question and to be embraced and adhered to with passion, knowing that the teaching came directly through the prophet. If this demand for obedience is not followed and ones actions become known, then that individual is considered an apostate and, in general, shunned by the leaders and membership of the church. In my case I was declared not only an apostate but a 'son of perdition.' There was a level of fear in my family that was palpable. It became so fierce that some prayed for my death so I could not be of influence to them or other members. They were, and still are, driven by fear.

All I did was declare that I loved them and was seeking truth like the church taught. I found that the teaching of Universal Truth, as taught by that church, was not to be found anywhere in the church. The challenge for them was that they could not penetrate the Love I showed them in spite of all the power and authority behind the religion. They could not, through all their power, prophets, and authority, touch me, spiritually or physically. I will move on to the next level of existence when it is destined.

Blind Faith-Blown Out Of Proportion

Blind faith has always been demanded by all world religions and, throughout the history of Christianity and Islam, has been the cause of millions of deaths, up to and including the present day. The wars being perpetrated today are a result of religious beliefs. Religion being the aggressor on one hand and the defender on the other. Our political leaders can claim it is due to the free worlds need for petroleum but the passionate religious beliefs of both sides are the root cause.

Spirit can be, and is accessed through the individuals heart. It is all around us and in us. Spirit exists because of love. Spirit is not aggressive. It is not religion nor doctrine. It cannot be spread through religion. It can only be shared by each individual caring for humankind. Spirit is action. Spirit is Love. There is nothing blind about it. It can be seen, felt, and experienced.

When we change from the worlds conditioning of our minds and lives and put our passion in seeking Spirit, Love, and Source, we un-complicate our lives and become calm and peaceful. What has been a cloud over our mind and vision of daily life is dispersed and we connect with true reality not the three dimensional one.

Chapter 14

Guides & Messengers

DSC05233 3/28/11 5:17:03PM

One of two Guides/Messengers that appeared at the same time. Higher Entities delivering messages.

The orbs in the trees beneath this messenger have content and life and always accompany the Entities as they deliver their messages of comfort, support, and Love.

Even though years have passed since these messengers appeared, I still feel great comfort when I look upon this, as well as other photographs I have taken. I will go into a meditative state while focusing on the picture and these higher dimensional Lifeforms. I always receive a message when seeing this, sometimes accompanied by the view of a higher place emanating beautiful streams of light that I can only describe as Love.

This entity was not visible to the natural eye. As the light from my strobe filled the night sky we witnessed it flying in a direction toward the natural forest that surrounded our home.

This lifeform, as well as countless others, keeps a constant vigil on nature and feeds back information to an invisible grid that encompasses Mother Earth. The grid communicates all necessary information both negative and positive so if action is needed to assist the Earth it is known instantly, not just in this frequency but others as well, also to higher dimensions including the Akashic Record where all information can be accessed. Assistance, as needed, occurs instantly. People in the world are unaware of this network of Love that protects our Home. Man generally takes credit for coming to the aid of the area affected when a tragedy is stopped or averted. These interdimensional rescue workers assist us without us even knowing it. If we were not blinded by our own knowledge and fascination of 3 dimensional technology we would be able to see and interact with them. They never ask for reward or credit. They do it out of Love for us and Earth.

This Lifeform is a Creator, and a protector of its' creations. It can transform and emulate other lifeforms including humankind. Creating also involves the imparting of knowledge to its' creations.

It appeared to me in the night sky to make its' presence known as part of my awakening in regards to the innumerable lifeforms that exist and are visiting Earth and assisting it, and us, in Ascension. The creation process is ongoing and this Creator has been involved from the beginning of this Earth.

I have not been taught the entirety of this Creators mission. More will be revealed in the future. The Awakening process cannot be assigned a time element. It is ongoing and in mankind's limited mental capacity it would seem to cover an eternity. Time is irrelevant, however the Awakening begins while Consciousness inhabits the physical body or vehicle.

This Transporter Lifeform appeared regularly over the same three month period each night one week before and after the full moon in 2013 and 2014. It creates ideas and concepts and projects them into working form. They function throughout various Universes. It is an intelligent entity.

These entities are also OVL's,(Organic Vehicles of Light). They are biological and can encompass other lifeforms to transport them to specific locations. They are helpful and will be recognized and photographed by others in the future.

There are six spheres inside each extension. The OVL can enlarge, if needed, to encompass larger spheres. Some transporters have as few as two tubular extensions, or arms, while I have photographed those with as many as six. They always encompass six spheres in each extension. The spheres in this picture are large enough to receive an entity, even a human, which can be transported to its' desired location, dimension, or frequency.

This transporter is dis-charging the spheres from one of its' arms. Five have been delivered and the sixth is in process. The lifeforms brought here by the OVL's are of a higher vibration and will remain with us as long as we want them to assist us. The communication between them and us is through telepathy or thought-projection. While many are coming to assist, many more are coming just to observe the process we are going through.

This OVL has delivered its' passengers and will return when they have completed their mission.

A lifeform can, in itself, come, or appear in the shape of a sphere or orb. This photograph clearly shows an entity within the sphere. This craft shows clear details or designs on its' surface. The craft is generating its own energy. It is a creation of thought. It is not of this physical realm. Higher frequency is present in the field immediately around the craft. This entity has come to observe and will show itself to other individuals as they tune in to this specific frequency. It is benevolent in nature and very loving. It is here to assist, observe, as well as learn from us.

IMG_6957 5/30/14 8:44:08pm

With the world being conditioned the way it has been, we very rarely look up to the heavens. We are more concerned in making it through the day, worrying about our daily chores and being able to make the house payment. When we adjust our priorities, putting our energy towards caring for Earth, Creation, and our Higher Consciousness we can easily observe what is happening all around us. We are being watched over, observed, assisted, cheered-on and greatly loved by those of our true family whom exist in many Dimensions and Universes.

IMG_3185 5/24/13 10:55:09pm

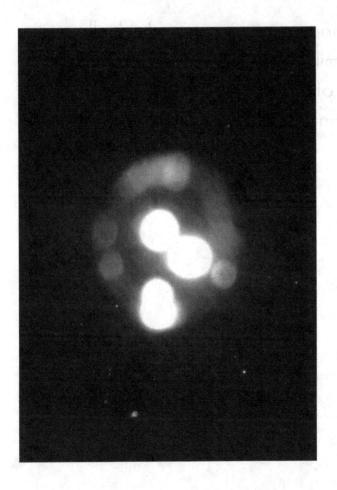

There are entities that have evolved and never incarnated on the Earth plane. They explore the Universes, observe and process information from other lifeforms and inhabited planets in many varied frequencies.

This group of entities, though individuals by creation, are unified in their desire to learn and evolve.

They may choose to incarnate, individually or as a group or 'family' in the future. It is not uncommon for groups of lifeforms to be together. They learn from, and assist each other in their desire to progress.

This infra-red photo shows holographic projections that originated on the moon. The three projections to the left migrated further as I observed the process. They eventually settled in the same formation as the three stars that form the belt of the Constellation Orion.

This is not an uncommon event. I have photographed it on many occasions, as well as other events that I will write about in the future.

Conclusion: The moon is a Probe placed in orbit around Earth, in most cases to help and assist us. It is also inhabited by physical lifeforms with their own agenda, but, can no longer use their knowledge of more advanced technology to play the games they have over the past millennia. Their hands, per se, have been tied while the event of disclosure and Ascension is under way. Nothing in the Universe is as powerful as Love.

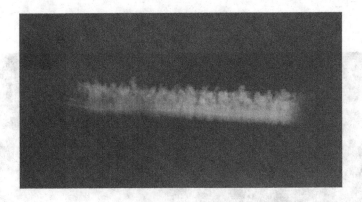

This object appeared to me and identified itself as a fifth dimensional creation. It is a vehicle with many Master entities. They travel together to teach those who are to excel in their fields of study. They are here to teach specific humans, also those visitors who have come from other dimensions that require their wisdom.

Although these Fifth Dimensional Masters are capable of appearing in physical form, they generally do not.

The two lines of Light seen over the full length of the craft are sensors. This vehicle is a carrier of those who contain and depart truths. Truths that are key to the human race. It is a great blessing that this vehicle is in our environment.

Different and varied, higher dimensional lifeforms
are regular visitors to our lower three dimensional
existence. They travel back and forth through
one of many gateways like this one in the area of
our Sun.

They are here to assist and oversee those who have come to observe and learn from our process of Awakening. They also observe those of humankind that have no desire to ascend at this time

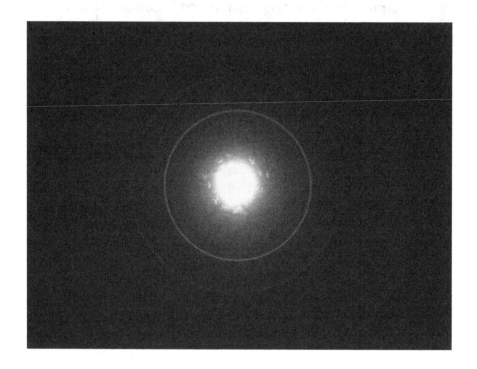

I was awakened at 3:30am one morning and encouraged to go outside and take pictures of the moon in infrared mode. One and a half hours, and more than 400 pictures later I sensed a closer bond with the lunar energy and noticed a curtain of unknowing had lifted from my mind and I had a higher understanding of the purpose and job description of this celestial 'probe'.

The Moon is inhabited by varying forms of life. Its' primary purpose is to monitor and assist the

Earth and its' inhabitants. Other cosmic lifeforms use it as a base or jumping off point as they further explore our area of the galaxy since they are not allowed to interfere with us any more.

DSC_02655 7/26/12 10:56:20am

This picture was taken during a surge in solar activity. The increased radiation could have been harmful to much of terrestrial life. This 'shield' between us and the Sun acted as a buffer protecting Earth from any potential harm. It lasted for several days. The membrane was created and placed there by Higher Dimensional Entities. Technology by the 'so called creator gods' was not employed. Had the creators of this shield not helped at this time the lesser creator gods would have been able to initiate a type of Armageddon they have woven into religious teachings of the world gaining a greater foothold in the continuing manipulation of humankind.

We are watched over, loved and protected by those Entities of higher vibration, frequency, and dimension.

There was no special attachment or filter used in this or any other of my photos. I simply point the camera using my intuition as the camera becomes more sensitive to my energy field. I simply take the picture and excitedly await the results on the viewing screen. At times I am aware of what the camera will produce, nevertheless, it is always exciting to produce the beauty of Life and Creation that appears each time I raise my camera to the Cosmos.

IMG_1917 3/10/12 6:32:09pm

A group of OVL's pass overhead during a light rainstorm. Their vigil and assistance is ongoing while we complete the process of Enlightenment to the remaining people of the Earth. Once the process is complete we will leave this 3 dimensional world and enter into the higher dimension with the Earth and leave behind those destined to continue their journey toward Enlightenment upon this or other worlds.

Chapter 15

Visions, Dreams, And
A Special Gift

A Column Of Angels

I awoke early one morning, looked over at my
wife, still asleep, then laid my head back on the
pillow and entered my quiet world of meditation.
A scene opened to my view;

I was looking at a beautiful Tudor mansion in what appeared to be the English countryside. I wasn't walking, I just approached the large hand carved door. The detail was exquisite. I entered the mansion. The beautiful detail continued on into the interior. With my love and knowledge of woodworking and my background in historic restoration, I paid close attention to the trim and moulding throughout the main floor.

The window treatments were a compliment to the woodworking. The hardwood floors were covered with Persian rugs fit for a King.

I continued walking through a large hall-like ballroom that displayed a huge, hand detailed game table in the center. There were no chairs around it.

As I moved further into the structure I saw more of the same quality workmanship. What I also noticed was that no one had greeted me. The mansion was filled with people but they concealed themselves. I could feel their energy. They knew who I was and that I had a right to be there, as much a right as they had, yet I knew they wanted me to leave.

There was an air of intimidation felt by them upon my entering the magnificent structure.

I moved across the ballroom, through a wide open doorway, to the back of the mansion. I walked up to a huge sliding glass door and was greeted by a view of rolling, emerald green hills accented from time to time with huge ancient Oaks and an occasional hedge-row of a darker green yet equally as beautiful as the emerald hills. The event was breathtaking, and I knew I had moved into a higher dimension as I opened the glass door and exited the mansion.

I noticed some people had gathered at a small lake in the distance. There were no trees immediately around the lake yet it was equally beautiful as the green hills rolled down into it.

As I got closer I noticed the people were all looking toward the heavens. I didn't look up until I reached the crowd. As I did I saw, immediately above the lake, an iridescent cloud in the shape of a ring with an inner cross like a compass. Immediately beneath the cross, at the center of the circle was, what I would describe, a column of four higher lifeforms, one above the other. I describe them as Angels because they had what appeared to be wings, although folded, that extended well above their heads.

As I looked upon the scene I knew I was witnessing something symbolic, from the Creator, but the full interpretation of this scene would come over a longer period of time. I absorbed the beauty and power of the experience as I continued to gaze upon it.

The 'Entities' were not clothed in woven fabric robes, they were clothed in the same iridescence as the circular cloud above them. Their hair, faces, and wings were, likewise, iridescent. The only part of their countenance that was different were their eyes.

The eyes of the first, second and fourth Angel were brighter than the brightest sun as they looked straight into my eyes. I was not blinded, but saw them clearly. I looked into the third Angels eyes. They were black. He also was looking into my eyes. In the magnificence of the moment I wondered what it all meant.

When I had been walking through the mansion I knew precisely what was happening, and what it meant. I knew the building represented the world and that I was not wanted there. I also knew that those worldly influences could not deter me, nor harm me in any way. The inhabitants of the mansion were greatly intimidated and afraid.

I knew the compass like cloud represented Supreme Creator, Source, and that there was a direct connection between Source and the four Entities.

Before the scene closed I was shown that the fourth Entity was me, in this lifetime. I would get confirmation about the others several years later.

I opened my eyes and found myself back in my bed. I looked at the clock. It was 5:30 a.m

The Ancient Ones

Eight years later I received a visit from "the Ancients Ones" and was told that the other three 'Angels' represented three other lifetimes I had experienced upon this Earth. They confirmed what I had felt. I was told that this would be the final lifetime before a final Ascension. The lake, or body of water beneath the column, represented the multi dimensional existence of humankind. Just like the photos I had taken of the Entities around the Sun, during the day, and the different lifeforms emanating light at night, and during storms, infinite life exists in the oceans and other bodies of water that cover this Earth and other spheres. The third 'Angel' looked at me with eyes that were black. The Ancients have shown me that black is the true color of Light, all else is a variation of it.

They stated that things are moving rapidly now. Time is not as it was!

With that, they departed and I was left once more with a magnificent display of Divine Light, forming beautiful arrangements and erupting into indescribable shapes and forms. They filled my Consciousness with what I can only describe as 'memories of home.'

He said, "You'll never make it to the top!"

Upon another occasion, entering that place in my private world of meditation, I found myself on what appeared to be a Greek island. I was at the harbor of a village that rose from the beautiful azure blue sea up the slopes of a mountain several hundred feet. Behind the village the mountain ascended several thousand feet higher. I knew I was to climb to the summit.

I began my ascent when I noticed there was no one in sight. Still I knew I had to complete my journey. There was no way to go around due to the sheer cliffs at either end of the town. There were no paths or alleyways to help me move up the terraced village landscape.

I looked for an open door hoping I could easily move up to the next terrace. There was none. I immediately, without hesitation, began to scale one of the white stuccoed dwellings until I reached the terra cotta tiled roof. I continued up to the peek and examined the next cobblestone street and row of houses at the next level. It was vacant as the first. I jumped down from the roof and began climbing onto the next row of terraced houses, all connected to one another. I repeated the climb up several terraces when I found myself standing on the peek of the forth row of dwellings.

I scanned the view of the beautiful harbor below and the contrast between the seas magnificent blue expanse and the vivid white stucco and red tile roofs of the dwellings I had been ascending. I began to go down the back side of the roof when I heard a movement behind me. I turned and saw a man coming toward me. A striking man in his thirties with blond hair and piercing blue eyes.

As he got closer to me he said in a threatening voice, "You'll never make it to the top!"

I said nothing. I simply raised my arm and pointed at him, as he continued toward me. He immediately stopped as though he had run into an invisible wall. He quickly turned, and scurried back down the way he came, defeated. I turned and continued my ascent until I reached the summit.

Although the town was vacant and no one appeared to assist me to make my ascent easier, I drew upon the strength, the power within me, to continue my climb. As the opposition made its presence known and declared my eventual defeat before reaching the summit, I drew upon that power within and rebuked the man, and completed my Ascension. In like manner I will complete my journey through this 'cycle of life' until my Ascension is complete.

This is the message I am to share with those throughout the world that find themselves challenged in the same way. The strength, the power to continue in reaching the fullness of your creation, your destiny, lies within. No one person, organization or government has the power to keep you from 'making it to the top,' unless you relinquish that power to them. Even if you have, a power still exists within you to take it back.

A Gift

Leaving my family behind in Uruguay when I was 16 to attend high school in Southwest Wyoming was difficult at first but also exciting, an adventure for such a young person.

My parents had given me a sound foundation. I knew right from wrong, at least the Mormon right from wrong. I stayed out of trouble and remembering the stories my father told me from my childhood about the Wind River Mountains, I was anxious to survey the surrounding desert and eroded plateaus near where I lived. It was a desolate landscape yet beautiful in its own way. I can still smell the fresh cool sage impregnated breeze sweeping across the desert after a spring or summer shower.

My new best friend, Leonard, loved to explore like me. We would load up his '52 Ford pickup and head out to the desert every chance we could get.

We surveyed ancient Indian campsites, looked for Dinosaur bones and petrified trees. Once we came upon fossilized turtle shells. They were sticking out of the eroded side of a small plateau.

On one of our weekend treks we were looking for more 'treasures' to collect. Leonard headed several hundred yards to the South while I scaled the side of a small plateau. I walked across the flat summit for several minutes with my eyes focused on the ground looking for arrowheads, agates, fossils, whatever looked unusual and out of place with the terrain. As I began descending the other side of the plateau I slid in the loose eroded gravel like soil. I put out my hands to catch myself while sliding, then immediately popped back up continuing my descent. As I continued descending I felt an artifact in my left hand. I stopped in my tracks, opened my hand and there saw a perfectly shaped object of what I assumed was obsidian. It had obviously been worked by hand and represented something, but what? It was a seemingly insignificant event, yet I felt something different, something otherworldly in my immediate surroundings. The feeling did not subside.

The artifact stayed with me throughout the years, in fact, I still have it in my possession to this day. It has traveled with me to the many third world countries I have lived in. I have shown it to few people. I have felt protective of it and in many ways its guardian. The very moment it appeared in my hand, more than 50 years ago, still remains fixed in my heart as though it was this morning.

A friend visited our home recently at our invitation. I reviewed many of the Lightstorm photographs with her. After we dined I felt I needed to share with her some of the artifacts I have been given over the years. She immediately felt the energy and meanings of some artifacts given me from Tiwanaku, Bolivia many years ago. She told a bit of their ancient history and that they are much older than archaeologists dare to believe.

I was excited to show the obsidian artifact but said nothing of how it came into my possession. She said that it had been brought here from off this planet but that it originated here and was taken away. It was brought to me as a gift and would teach me many things about the Universe, Light, and the Cosmos. The artifact, she said, is hundreds of thousands of years old and that it contained much information. I told her how it came into my possession and the extraordinary circumstances surrounding it. She smiled.

I have been given some of the knowledge it is to share. It shows in its very shape what some ancient theorists would claim as the profile of an Extraterrestrial species.

Exposing The Great Lie!

As we go through life we absorb a treasure of experiences. We are perfect creations. Our Consciousness is receiving this precious knowledge that can only be experienced through incarnation. It has been the goal of those entities hungry for, and blinded by, power to control this world. Humanity has been deceived in believing it is not in control of its own existence and can only follow the accepted norms of society to advance. This is a lie!

This is, and has been through three other lifetimes, what I am here to teach. We are all connected. No one is greater than the other. There are some more enlightened than others, but no greater than others.

As a person 'awakens', it is by choice, not by chance. It is a conscious decision to look for, to seek answers. They are awaiting you.

Awakening From Conditioning

Religion is an influence that comes from the outside in. Belief comes from outside the heart. Feelings created in the body change our environment. When we take beliefs into our heart we create our environment based on those feelings that are now influencing the world around us. They affect our world and our interests, our spouse, our children, our friendships, our work environment, everything and everyone we interact with.

Becoming informed through Universal Consciousness is receiving Knowledge and Wisdom from the Cosmos. This happens through accessing your Higher Self. It is not a belief system that you take into your Heart and mix with your emotions, it is perfect Knowledge that has come from your Higher Self. It is understanding, comprehending that you are an extension of Source.

As you experience this you learn about the wonderful gift that emotion is. Emotion is a servant to Consciousness and is directed to assist the individual in Ascension. Belief, on the other hand, when taken into the heart, becomes the emotion and directs the individual in the way it is to react. This has been the m.o. of religions, governments and people craving power during this current 'cycle of civilization'

Human emotion through Consciousness is what changes the world. It is not faith believing that it will happen. It is speaking as though it has already happened. The energy field around our heart creates the event as though it already is. We program ourselves to Ascension. If we don't ascend during this lifetime then we continue on to other worlds and lifetimes until we do.

This has been the message of the Sages throughout history. This for the most part, has been kept secret and hidden by those in positions of power, to keep it from mankind. Few of their teachings can be found in the Bible and the Torah. The majority of their teachings have been removed to more easily facilitate the indoctrination and manipulation of society and culture.

Many people throughout the Earth have had visions and dreams that were, and are to assist in their own Awakening. Many, though, have tried to interpret these dreams and visions through religious beliefs and indoctrinations. Many go to their ecclesiastical leader for an interpretation to that event that was meant solely for that individual. In doing so it gifts more authority to that religion or faith, strengthening the control it already has over the individual. The true understanding of the vision or dream is explained and then understood through accessing their own Higher Consciousness.

As with my own interdimensional experiences the answers may come instantly. Then again, they may only be partially answered at first, as was mine with the column of Angels, with the complete answer coming some time later.

Accessing higher Consciousness gives us the answers, not some of them, all of what we seek answers to is available to us.

Chapter 16

DNA

The reason we, as humankind, have been able to use only a portion of our brain power is because only two strands of our DNA have been active, until now, during this cycle of life.

On Earth where free-will is allowed, there also exists the possibility for more advanced intelligence, hidden in frequency, to program ways to manipulate humankind on this three dimensional plane. Free-will has been permitted at all levels in regards to the Earth. Love and Compassion are unknown to many of these beings of higher intelligence, not to be confused with higher dimensions, because they have not sought to take on physical bodies as we have. Living in a physical body is hard work and they have chosen to live off of the energy produced when we fall victims to fear they create through our emotions because it is easier for them as opposed to taking on a physical form. They want us to provide for them. They have lived off of our efforts and benefited themselves at our expense. They are now being exposed.

They have been tempted more by their abilities to manipulate and control humankind from behind frequency, cloaked in invisibility and feeding off the negative energy we emit from within our physical state.

They have maintained their power through our emotions, especially that of fear. Fear stunts our growth but nourishes theirs. Light is information and Light coming to this Earth has been controlled, or filtered, by these creator gods, until now.

As some 'higher intelligences' have willingly accepted the title of god from mankind in general and set up religions to promote their agenda, the time has come in the history of humankind, upon this Earth, to have the truth of these so called gods revealed. The contents of the Bible and the Koran have been cleverly manipulated and embellished and edited to strengthen their position, while along the way, throughout history, other key teachings and inspiring testaments have been declared heresy and stricken from these so called words of God that the world so readily and blindly accepts as irrevocable and indisputable truth, in their present state.

Some of the teachings of the Koran and the Bible are true and do assist in guiding us to the knowledge of ourselves, who we are, why we are here on this Earth at this time, and what we have come here to accomplish. Knowing how to ferret out this information is the key.

Junk DNA-Really?

Getting back to DNA. We have been shown that our DNA is a double helix that contains all the information to establish our identity and it has become the key in helping to trace our ancestry and identify 'imperfections' and 'genetic traits' as well as assist law enforcement in solving crimes. Science has found much more, however, and has not been able to unlock it, so has cleverly identified it 'junk DNA.' At least this is what we are being told!

The fascinating and recent discovery of a new, second DNA code further lends credence to what metaphysical scientists have been saying for millennia — the body speaks two different languages.

> "Since the genetic code was deciphered in the 1960s, researchers have assumed that it was used exclusively to write information about proteins.
>
> But biologists have suspected for years that some kind of epigenitic inheritance occurs

at the cellular level. The different kinds of cells in our bodies provide an example. Skin cells and brain cells have different forms and functions, despite having exactly the same DNA.

NOSUCHTHINGASJUNKDNA

The human genome is packed with at least four million gene switches that reside in bits of DNA that once were dismissed as "junk" but it turns out that so-called junk DNA plays critical roles in controlling how cells, organs and other tissues behave. The discovery, considered a major medical and scientific breakthrough, has enormous implications for human health and consciousness because many complex diseases appear to be caused by tiny changes in hundreds of gene switches.

As scientists delved into the "junk" — parts of the DNA that are not actual genes containing instructions for proteins — they discovered a complex system that controls genes. At least 80 percent of this DNA is active and needed. Another 15-17 percent has higher functions scientists are still decoding.

Recent findings in the journal Science may have big implications for how medical experts use the genomes of patients to interpret and diagnose diseases, researchers said.

The genetic code uses a 64-letter alphabet called codons. Dr Stamatoyannopoulos with co-authors were stunned to discover that some codons, which they called duons, can have two meanings. One describes how proteins are made, and the other instructs the cell on how genes are controlled."

www.universityof washington.edu

The human body speaks many languages in many dimensions and was initially created with 12 strands of DNA yet the medical world says there are only 2. That double helix represents 16.67% of our initial DNA of 12 strands. Like the inspiring teachings and testaments that have been hidden from the world, the other 10 strands have also been hidden. These strands are at this time being activated. It is not occurring in all those upon the earth. It can awaken all of humankind, but the key to this happening falls back on to free-will. There are those people that will look truth in the face and declare it does not exist, or that it is a lie and it is manipulation in its most heinous form to get the world to believe the great lie and steer us away from the 'perfect word of god.' How thorough has been the brainwashing through religion.

From time to time there have been Messengers sent from Supreme Creator to assist in awakening humankind to this dilemma. The creator gods could not be condemned for their actions since all is allowed in a free-will zone. However, Messengers could be sent to teach and awaken humanity, if humanity would be awakened.

An attempt was made 2000 years ago with positive results and people began to think for themselves. The results were disturbing to the Roman empire and the master teachers of that era would not be stopped. Rome did not want to kill these teachers because they would be declared martyrs and the movement would gain strength that even the Roman army could not withstand.

The greatest army in the world, at the time, had forcefully conquered all their enemies in battle, but this was different. This movement was not based on hatred, power and control. It was born out of Love. They witnessed what the power of Love was doing throughout their kingdom, and the empire had to do something or face losing their political power and thus control over the masses.

The mother of Emperor Constantine fell victim to the message of Love and made pilgrimages to Jerusalem and claimed to have located many sacred places that had been added to the story of Love. Stories were told, and embellished to give them more credence. People readily believed them because these stories gave them hope. Survival, hope, and faith are the only things possible to a world controlled through fear. Constantine was influenced by his mother and began to incorporate Christian beliefs into the Roman culture. A shrewd and brilliant political move. Over time he established a council to determine what would be scriptural and what would be heresy. The rest is now history.

Female Pastors--Unthinkable?

Historical research shows us that the majority of the teachers of this new movement were women. It also tells of the teaching of reincarnation. Reincarnation was taught with an emphasis on a Supreme Creator who loves us and has provided a way for us to return after having learned the lessons of Compassion and Love while in a physical body. This process would take multiple lifetimes to accomplish. Each lifetime teaching something not learned in the previous. However many incarnations it would take until Ascension was attained.

The power of the message of Love was manipulated, distorted, twisted and made into what was to become the most powerful religious and political movement this cycle of civilization has ever known.

Acts Of Power Not Love

Ascension was the teaching, not resurrection, at the time. Resurrection was introduced out of necessity, and religious and political control, by Constantine. The truth about reincarnation and Ascension was hidden. Women were declared unworthy to teach the doctrine in the 'Universal Church.' Reincarnation was declared heresy and the true teaching of Ascension was outlawed and replaced with the false doctrine of the resurrection. Ascension was achieved through many lifetimes. Resurrection was to be attained in just this lifetime if one lived a perfect life. If one did not live worthy of the resurrection they would be confined to purgatory or hell upon death. The masses were forced to accept these new declarations by the Nicean Council or face torture and even death. Ancestors who had died were already in purgatory but the living family members had the privilege of paying the priest to pray for them and light candles to assist the ancestors delivery from an eternity in hell.

The plan worked to perfection. The creator gods had circumvented a takeover by Love. They replaced it with intimidation, manipulation, and fear, also known as the Universal Church. What could not be stopped was an underground movement that continued. Many people have awakened to this here-to-for hidden knowledge. They are aware of, and able to receive, higher knowledge that has been available to us all throughout this present cycle of time. All we need to do is receive it. The Earth at this time is being showered with light from the Cosmos, including our Sun. This light is assisting in making active our dormant DNA. As we respond, our capacity to receive more Knowledge and Light increases. Light is Knowledge. Light is information.

Light Is Infinite

Light is infinite and so is our ability to receive it. All we have to do is choose to wake up.

The gods of history have had the ability to create, and assisted in the programing of the human body that we use as a vehicle to experience life on Earth. They helped create the human vehicle but had no input in the creation of Earth. Our Mother Earth, who loves us and provides for us, has been patiently awaiting us, expecting us to awaken and take our place as superiors to those creator gods. Now we know they are not gods but have been playing with us, manipulating us, controlling us at every turn throughout history. They have lacked the human emotion that we experience through these very bodies they helped design. Somewhere along the way they chose to exercise their egos over their hearts. They chose to exercise power over Compassion. They forgot that Love is what creation is all about. But then, they, like us, exercised their 'free-will.'

Supreme Creator, or Prime Creator, has intervened to help us remember who we are. With the assistance of other more benevolent creations and entities throughout this Galaxy, and the Universe, we are being given the opportunity to awaken to the awareness of who we are, Consciousness experiencing physical form.

Chapter 17

Activating Our Intent

In physical form we have had our hands tied for more than 6,000 years. Now we are being given the choice to wake up or continue on in ignorance. It still comes down to free-will. Our Consciousness is always aware and informed but we need to activate our intent to remember, in physical form, what Consciousness already knows.

What Consciousness does know is that, with our DNA fully made active, we become greater than the creator gods, who created the problem, due to our human experience. It is our turn to teach them Love and Compassion. To teach them that we progress faster when Love is the vehicle of choice rather than power and ego. Everyone benefits when we show Love and Compassion.

As we come out of the darkness we have been in for 6,000 years, we become the example for the Universe to follow in helping bring it to completion.

We Are Divine Creations

That is what we are doing now. Bringing ourselves, as divine creations, to completion. We are ascending along with the Earth. We will be able to move within higher dimensions and take a lighter, more perfect, ascended physical body with us. This is the Ascension I am referring to. This is the Ascension the Sages and Prophets of old taught about.

Some of these teachings can be found in the Old Testament as it is presented to the world today. Some of the teachings regarding reincarnation can also be found there. Very little of the New

Testament can be trusted as truth. The world loves to believe stories they cannot prove. The real history of Christianity is documented and is available to those who search. Jesus lived and died just like other mortals. He was not crucified. He did not resurrect and rise into heaven as told in the New Testament. His family tomb was unearthed in an area of Jerusalem in 1980 at which time his ossuary, along with other ossuaries of members of his family interred there, were placed in storage and kept from the world because of the effect that information might have on Christianity, and possibly even more damaging to the commercial and economical side of the religion. It would also give more credence to the Muslim world since they have declared him a prophet and messenger and nothing more.

This crucial information was finally, and quietly, leaked in 2008. Bones were recovered from the ossuary and possibly DNA. Along with the ossuary of Yeshua was that of his wife, his mother, and a son named Judah. News of this discovery has not been sensationalized by the media because they are afraid they would lose face, and ratings, due to what they feel would be a public outcry claiming lies and manipulation of the Christian story by the media. What the media is blind to is the real feeling of the common person. Many people when approached on the street declare that they don't even care any more. They are 'turned off' to religion. They feel there is something that has been hidden from them, not only by religion but by governments and by society itself, and they would be correct! All three are linked and have been part of the great deception, now being exposed!

The Antichrist

Of the three, religion is the great monster. The Book of Revelations in the New Testament talks about the Great Harlot being exposed in the last days. It speaks of the Antichrist and the destruction through power and control of a Christian world because of this entity, and only worthy Christians being saved or 'caught up' into the heavens while the earth is cleansed by fire, destroying, or consuming, all those unworthy.

These are interesting ideas and one who chooses to see the light finds that Christ is not a person but a calling to the master teachers throughout time. This message through 'Christ Consciousness' then touches the human heart because it is one of Love and Compassion and truly unconditional in its manifestation.

There was no Christ, but many throughout time with 'Christ Consciousness'. Then there can be no Antichrist other than religion itself. Religion as an entity, no matter what the doctrine or dogma, has been the root evil behind all wars throughout the past six millennia, and probably more. It has been the main vehicle used by the creator gods to manipulate and control humankind.

Interactive Holograms

One of the most important tools of the creator gods throughout human existence on Earth has been through the use of 'interactive holograms'. They have created many holographic sequences and inserted them into our frequency, to play out fake events and change the course of our history to their liking. All of these holograms have been tied to historic religious events.

Visions of the Virgin Mary throughout history have played, probably, the greatest role in promoting Christianity and in manipulating people the world over. These have been, for the most part, interactive holograms. Others have been mere inventions of the human mind, lies!

One of the most fascinating stories involving the creator gods and holograms has to be in the organizing and founding of the church I was born into.

Fourteen year old Joseph Smith, its founder, found himself in a grove of trees in upstate New York in 1820. He was evidently praying to know which church of all the many was the true church. A light descended upon him from the sky and he claimed to see two men in the column of light. He said they introduced themselves as God the Father, and his Beloved Son, Jesus Christ. They told him that none of the churches at the time were the true church and that he, Joseph, would be the instrument through which God would restore the 'true' church to the Earth that had been taken away from the Earth at the death of the twelve apostles from Bible lore.

As the years passed, Joseph Smith received many visitations from 'heavenly messengers' claiming to give him the authority, or priesthood, to fully restore the previously fallen church. He claimed to have been visited by Adam, Enoch, Moses, Elijah, John the Baptist and others, also claiming that he received the keys of the restoration giving him, and only him, literally, the power of heaven upon earth.

Other visitors included Moroni, an ancient American Prophet who delivered a collection of gold plates upon which a history of the ancient American inhabitants was written in 'reformed Egyptian,' a script known only to the ancient American Prophet and his father, Mormon. In 421 a.d. the gold plates were hidden in a stone box in a hill not far from the Smith family farm near Palmyra, New York. The name of the hill, according to the 'Angel Moroni', was Cumorah.

After four years of proven faithfulness, Joseph was given possession of the gold plates to translate into what today is known as the Book of Mormon. Only a small handful of men were able to see and witness, in writing, of their existence. Some even claimed to have seen the angel Moroni. Sometime shortly thereafter Joseph Smith gave the plates back to Moroni for safe keeping.

It is a fascinating collection of 'angelic manifestations' and can be very compelling to someone who is not awakened, or partially awakened. An interesting note to the story is the existence of the chain of islands in the Indian Ocean just northwest of Madagascar. It is a group of beautiful islands similar to those of the Caribbean. What is of interest is the name of one of the Island groups, The Comoros. The capitol of The Comoros Islands is called Moroni. An interesting coincidence? These Islands have maintained these names for over 800 years, more than 600 years prior to the 'Restoration' of the 'true' church. Not only did the creator gods create the Mormon deception, they did it with a sense of humor.

The world today is much different than it was 50 years ago, even some 25 years ago when I separated myself from religion. I knew in my bones that I had been deceived regarding truth as I was taught. Not that my teachers were bad people. To the contrary, they were dedicated educators teaching what they had been conditioned to believe and what they had been taught was truth.

My parents were two of the most noble people in my life. I have the deepest love and respect for them and their dedication to the seven children they raised. My father teaching me to follow my heart and love God was the greatest thing he could have instilled in me.

It was a tremendous shock to him when I left the church yet he knew I was following my own heart and walking a path that only I could walk. He confided in one of my sisters that he didn't understand what had happened with me. He couldn't comprehend it, but he felt in his heart and declared with a calmness that all would be well in the end.

I sought truth at every opportunity and studied the Mormon religion in great depth until I physically separated myself from it. I didn't just wake up all of a sudden. I had been confident for many years prior that I would leave one day. I didn't know exactly where it would lead me but I couldn't live with my feelings about it and remain any longer. I had been anticipating my door of opportunity for many years. It appeared and I walked through it with great joy and anticipation. I have never looked back.

It took some years to be able to put into words just what I was feeling at the time. I needed to understand the process I had been going through for the majority of my life, up until that time, not only as an adult but as a child and adolescent. I had been looking for answers all my life. What I came to realize was that I was awakened in my childhood. My DNA seemed to be more active than my peers, from infancy, yet I was required to experience religion from the inside, to know the doctrines, politics, and ins-and-outs of that organization. It is one of the most successful organizations in history. The members are, for the most part, very dedicated and honest in their dealings. There are always exceptions.

The fact that I left the church and was excommunicated still does not give me license to defame or degrade it. I simply wanted to know what was behind all religion since it was the cause of so much human suffering while at the same time teaching that it is only through religion that one can go to heaven.

Many Are Awakening

The truth is, millions are awakening to what is going on in the world today. No one has to attack religion to destroy it. Religion is devouring itself from within. The creator gods time has passed, so to speak. Humankind is getting the input (light) it has sought for thousands of years. Our full DNA is being made active. We are the messengers of light promised in the scriptures.

Chapter 18

Holograms

Our definition of a hologram is; a three dimensional image formed by the interference of light beams from a laser or other coherent light source. A coherent light source consists of waves having a constant phase relationship.

Light is in all things and, in fact, is all things. We are learning to live in a body of flesh and bone that is made of Light, although at a very low vibrational level. This is known in the scientific world.

We are able to organize, or focus Light in a very limited fashion. Our approach to the understanding of light and its function has been from a platform of three dimensional, low vibrational technology. Archaic to say the least. Higher vibrational intelligence works at a higher level of technology. It is more sophisticated at higher levels. That does not mean from higher dimensions. Higher vibrational levels exist within the third and fourth dimensions. We, in most cases, do not knowingly interact with these vibrations, yet we have been victims of much of this manipulative technology.

Holograms are used by fifth dimensional beings, benevolent entities, however, they are always used to teach us while three dimensional technology is used, in great part, to deceive and manipulate humankind. The key word being technology. Technology is not associated with fifth dimensional interaction. Messages and holographic interaction are created through, and by light. There is nothing to construct as in the lower dimensions. The higher dimensions create through intent and through sound vibration.

In a sense, speaking whatever is required into existence.

Even at the deceptive level of holographic technology, many people are not capable of noticing the difference. That is why so much interference has been successful throughout the past several millennia. The only physical way one can distinguish the difference is through vibration. To the intuitive person this vibration is not pure. The vibration and frequency in itself is manipulated to create and introduce the hologram. It is changed.

Holographic UFO's

Many of the UFO's seen in the sky over the millennia have not been actual manufactured craft. What they have been are manufactured Holograms projected into our frequency, generally to deceive and promote intimidation and fear. Over the past few decades our 'shadow' government has obtained the technology to fabricate many of these UFO holographic projections, exchanging favors for designs used in the manufacturing of the holographic projectors. Individuals within our own frequency, or vibration, are programming 'events' of discovery by an ignorant population pronouncing statements giving credit to aliens from other worlds when they have originated right here, mostly underground in the USA. One more recent event of their making is the Phoenix UFO phenomenon.

Some people who have witnessed UFOs have claimed to feel a strange vibration or interruption in the immediate surrounding. This is evidence of the manipulation of vibration/frequency. It causes fear in the participant and disrupts the natural flow of energy in the individual. It has been known to stay with some witnesses throughout their entire life. It causes wonder, tied in with fear. Fear is what the creators of this type of phenomena live on, literally. Fear is energy. Energy produced through fear is nutrition to the false gods of creation. It gives them control over mankind who are, at times working with knowing individuals in our frequency infatuated in the knowledge and working relationship they have with these intradimensional beings, and have been doing so at times throughout this 'cycle of life.' Without a constant flow of the frequency of fear they cannot control.

Holographic Messengers

Many of these holograms have been 'interactive,' in other words, people have been able to interact with them, touching them, feeling what appears to be solid, and at times becoming ill from the experience, but not always.

Joseph Smith, the Mormon prophet explained how 'heavenly messengers' laid hands on his head and through that ritual transferred the 'keys of heaven' to him, giving him all the power needed to establish the Mormon religion. Many other interactive holographic visions have been recorded by pious women and men throughout the history of religion. Most, if not all, were honorable people, including children, and the religious, superstitious masses believed these events. It is understandable why people believed. With centuries, even millennia, of conditioning and manipulation by the creator gods and their mortal proxies, i.e: inspired, political and ecclesiastical leaders, as well as some royalty, there was little else for them to believe in.

The Supreme Creator sent teachers throughout our history to plant seeds of truth and give us direction, not to force us to change but invite us to. Enough to help inspire those along the way that were searching for answers, why the world is this way, and how one could have a true relationship with Source.

By Their Fruits

Many of the Old Testament prophets were among these Sages. In fact, Supreme Creator incarnated Itself in the guise of some of these Sages, teaching, leading, guiding, but never through manipulation or fear. They were known by their fruits, their teachings.

Many of the Old Testament stories have been embellished and some events added to or deleted from the Bible. One example is in the book of Exodus where Moses is credited with giving the House of Israel the Ten Commandments and all the regulations that accompanied them as recorded in the Torah, having received them directly from God.

Every society throughout history has needed rules and regulations to live by. Order is always needed but should never be enforced through anything but understanding, Compassion when needed, and yes, Love. Supreme Creator has, at no time, issued commandments to any culture, tribe or society. Earth is a free-will creation. Commandments and laws have always come from mankind and the creator gods, never from Supreme Creator. We are here to learn, to experience life in these mortal bodies, to experience emotion to learn to control our fear, to exercise Love and Compassion and to look for answers . . . answers that will exalt us, lift us up to an understanding of who we are, the perfect creations that we are, along with Consciousness.

Earth Ascending

As the Earth is ascending in its vibration and preparing to enter the fifth dimension, the use of holographic inserts will increase. Those holograms associated with the lower vibrations, mostly through creator gods and 'shadow government', will be accompanied by chaos, hatred, control, and war. This can be witnessed every day throughout the Middle East as well as in cities across the globe where crime and gang, or tribal war mentality has broken out. We find much of this originating in the US and being exported abroad. It hasn't all come from the Middle East.

What is now required is for those in the United States, and other countries, to increase in the Awakening, to stand and be counted with those noble Souls already on the battle front with the support and momentum of our Cosmic family members here to assist. Showing and witnessing the 'Lightstorm' of Love, Compassion, and Universal Community.

Holographic teachings from higher vibrations are associated with the fifth dimension and will always be accompanied by harmony, peace, understanding and direction, all given to us through Love, never through force.

The Power Of The Mind

In the 1970's a man was being studied in a laboratory in Colorado. He was able to create a street scene of activity in front of himself. The scene could not be seen by the human eye. The scene could, however, be viewed in photographs taken of him. Rather than viewing his portrait in the developed photograph, the scene that he was focusing on in his mind appeared instead.

We are capable of creating partial holograms with our minds. The creator gods cannot since they are not incarnate. They have to do it through technology. In the Ascension process we increase in our abilities to create and project holograms without technology. We will become fully capable upon entering fifth dimensional reality.

This is only a small part of what the mind/ Consciousness is capable of. We have been envied by our creator gods because of the creative powers we have within us. They were aware, in the beginning, of the creation of the human form and that we could surpass them in our ability to create in association with Consciousness if we awakened, so they manipulated our DNA. They would need to activate two strands with the remaining ten hidden and inactive.

With only 16.67% of our DNA active we have been able to do some amazing things, and with the added assistance of the Sages throughout time, some of humankind has been able to awaken, activating their own DNA, in part at least. These individuals have been more aware of the power of the human creation and the power of thought.

In The Night Sky

In my infrared photography of the moon, in the darkness around it, there is a type of hieroglyphic writing in the night sky. This 'writing' is a result of thought. Our thoughts are our creation. We create them and send them out into the Cosmos. They are real and occupy space. These thoughts are good and bad. Humankind has been responsible for all of them in this area of the Galaxy. The majority of these thought forms are negative.

The creator gods have fed off of this negativity since they helped create the present model of human. They did not create Consciousness, only assisted in the creation of this physical body where Consciousness resides to experience life. Those creators knew the capability of the human lifeform, that it had the ability, when fully activated, to supersede their own abilities of creation.

I have often thought that they were limited in their abilities due to their laziness. Earlier in my life I assumed that laziness was connected to emotion. I since have discovered that laziness is a choice. The creator gods chose to play their games hidden behind frequency. They organized humankind to perform all the physical work while they reaped the benefits of our efforts. Doing their best to keep us isolated and controlled hoping we would never discover their games. They can no longer keep us in the dark. Ignorance is now a choice as the

Awakening is spreading throughout the Earth. We have created types of holograms using our own minds without knowing it but Consciousness knows. With interaction of our fifth dimensional Guides and Messengers no machine is required when done in a highly positive vibratory field. What more can humankind create as our DNA is fully made active.

I have had people approach me and insist they have met me, even conversed with me, about Enlightenment. Some years ago I was visiting a friend in Evansville, Indiana. We were conversing when we were interrupted by a man who was amazed at the coincidence of seeing me there when he had just met me the day before in a city two hundred miles to the North, a city I had never been to. I explained that he had probably seen someone looking similar to me and that I had never been there. He raised his voice to the point of anger wondering why I would lie about something like that when I was clearly the same person with the same features, voice, and mannerisms. I excused myself as he also turned and walked away frustrated to the point of anger that I would not acknowledge our meeting. At the time I didn't know about interactive holograms nor about multidimensional beings. We are more than what we see in the mirror.

It is much easier to see how we can ascend as we learn to use our minds in positive thinking. It is imperative that humankind gain control over the body. It is necessary to Love ourselves so we can Love others, respect ourselves so we can respect others. Even with just two strands of DNA active we can begin to activate the remaining through intent. We are being assisted by higher, more benevolent lifeforms. Entities who understand the power of the human creation. This, along with our desire to better ourselves, to rise above our present state and destructive nature, is what will allow the Earth to complete its Ascension, and we along with it.

The use of holograms is like the internet. They can be used for manipulative purposes both positive and negative. We can learn to 'read' the vibration to know whether it is from a good or a negative source as well as project our own holograms on higher, more positive vibrations. Many people have been doing just that for some time. That is why there is a wave of higher Intelligence in the varied lifeforms here now to assist and encourage us.

The use of holograms by benevolent entities will assist in triggering our DNA to action. The experience spurs us on to do more and act in a more loving way to others. The Ascension is an individual accomplishment but is accelerated as we share what we learn with humankind.

Beyond Disclosure

While much of the First World is anticipating the revelation by governments of the official existence of UFO's and extraterrestrial life, people are concentrating on what they feel the government should or shouldn't do while failing to notice what is happening all around them.

In the overall picture of existence much has been revealed and is visible to those who know where and how to view it.

Wherever Life Can Exist Life Does Exist!

Our government is partially aware of some of the higher technology available and has made use of it in some cases. This information of higher three dimensional technology has been and continues to be used in the distribution of misinformation and the spreading of lies laced with bits of truth to keep the American public, and the rest of the world, guessing. If we choose to listen and believe what is released by them and other entities bent on continuing global dominance, we continue to fall victim to their web of fear and deceit.

In actual fact the governments only know a fraction of what is available. One major key is knowing where and how to seek information. Mankind has been manipulated and misinformed through intradimensional contact, with only a small amount of truth intertwined with what is mostly lies meant to deceive. Finding Truth involves looking beyond what is physically visible and training yourself to tune in to the vibratory fields that exist all around us. Life is interdimensional and within each dimension exists frequencies and vibrations, at times overlapping. Life exists in all these fields. It exists in infinite shape and form. Every thing that exists is, in fact, alive. It is all Energy, Light.

An easy way to see life in another frequency is to begin using a camera. Cameras display a sensitivity to frequency, at least to some frequencies. You will probably be surprised at what appears in an area of the sky that you thought contained nothing more than clouds as it appears on your digital camera screen. Some daytime shots, using a strobe, contain Orbs but will become more visible in night photography. UFO's can be photographed the same way. While pointing the camera towards the sun and triggering the video mode, using a tripod, I have videoed UFO's on many occasions dancing in and out of the scene around the sun. At times other lifeforms will fly, in an uncommon way, in and out of the scene.

The more you attempt to connect with other lifeforms through higher intent, the more they will appear to you. You may be sitting in your favorite recliner, reflecting on Life that has appeared in your photos when a small ball of light appears from behind you moving at a rather quick pace as you view it disappear through the wall in front of you.

My wife had gone to help take care of the grandchildren for several days. I wanted to do something special for her so decided to upgrade our bedroom to a more romantic color while rearranging the furniture to correspond with what information I was receiving through higher Consciousness. After two days of work and planning, I completed it. The bedroom had a completely different feel to it. Much more positive and romantic. I couldn't wait for her to get home so I called to let her know what I had done and to help increase her level of excitement and anticipation. It worked! She asked me to take a picture and send it to her. I did. As the flash went off on the camera I saw the bedroom filled with Energy. Orbs/Spheres were moving throughout the room. It increased our level of excitement even more and we enjoyed each others anticipation upon her return.

Share

Share your knowledge and talents with wisdom. Become greater than the creator gods. Be one with Prime Creator. The time and energy spent in sharing what you experience with others will return to you many times over and will literally assist you further in your Awakening.

Chapter 19

Interdimensional Assistance

Life is infinite and resides in many different frequencies and dimensions. We are connected to all Life since we emanate from the same Source. The size of the Universe does not negate that fact. Though we Earthlings are in the dark regarding our past and origins due to the vail shrouding this 'cycle of existence,' not all Life out there is ignorant to what has occurred and is still occurring on Earth. Many want to help us by coming here, showing their desire to assist us towards Enlightenment.

They come in many different forms and vehicles. They have not openly disclosed their presence since mankind is so impregnated with fear, fear of attack and enslavement by a more ruthless alien lifeform as we have been conditioned to think by officials and perhaps, more so, Hollywood. Neither have they completely hidden themselves. They have always been accessible to those seeking truth about the Universe and our place in it.

One of the most important things I can reveal is that negativity and evil do not ultimately control this Earth. Ultimately Compassion and Love envelope our Earth and its inhabitants. No extraterrestrial power of any kind will be allowed to damage or destroy us. We are at a junction where mankind is damaging and destroying much of life, killing innocence, attempting to force the entire world to accept its demands. This wicked effort to force others to accept its dogma is no different from the evil spirit of the 'inquisition' that resulted in the deaths of millions of innocent people in both hemispheres during the 1300s' to 1600s'.

Those who practice Compassion and Love are directing their Energy and efforts towards blocking the ruthless advance of evil. Extraterrestrials have never been the problem. Creator gods, hidden in frequency, right here among us, along with those of mankind who demand to remain in power, are the problem. Creator gods are not extraterrestrials, they are intraterrestrials, right here among us.

I have been shown, and allowed to photograph, some of the varied vehicles of transport for those benevolent Lifeforms eager to come and assist. As I have previously mentioned they are not here to do it for us, but to enlighten us as to our place in the Cosmos. In doing so it allows us to view the beauty of our creation and the ultimate goal of our Ascension to higher dimensions.

Many people will not desire Ascension at this time. Many are, and will continue to be caught up in the drama of evil and destruction, perhaps through many more lifetimes, until they choose to awaken in their hearts, but, while here at this time, they will not be allowed to freely disrupt the movement to Enlightenment as it continues to assist those throughout the Earth that are intent upon their Awakening.

Transporter Rings & OVL's

Lifeforms have been coming to Earth for many years now. A wave came in the 1940s'. More in the 1970s', 80s' and 90s'. The greatest number so far have come in only recently. They come from different worlds, solar systems, galaxies and dimensions. They are aware of the need on Earth at this time to help humankind heal this planet before we go too far. These are benevolent lifeforms here to assist us in ascending in our thinking and our actions. They are aware of, and able to move through space and time, as we know it, to come here.

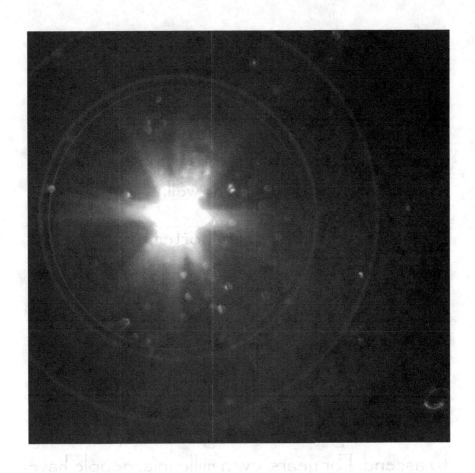

Some come individually, others come in groups. The area around the Sun in this photo, is a Portal between galaxies and dimensions. The thin rings around the sun work in harmony with the hexagon. The hexagon has evolved into its present form. When I began photographing the sun the field around it was originally in the shape of a square. The camera and settings have always been the same. What is important to know is that the energy within the hexagon, in conjunction with the rings, make up the Gateway or Portal that the smaller, ring shaped transporters enter and leave through. Those benevolent entities aboard these OVL's come here to be with us at this place and time. The other Orbs in this photograph contain, and transport other lifeforms, as well.

This photograph of Transporter Rings was the first of many I took beginning in 2012.

This photo represents only a portion of the multitude of Lifeforms existing in other dimensions and galaxies. They are here to assist humankind. Their purpose is solely to support and encourage us in assisting with those preparing to ascend. For years, even millennia, people have prayed for deliverance from physical, spiritual, and emotional bondage. Most have done so thinking it would come through religion, others through politics or governments. Neither is true. Varied lifeforms are here and more are coming. There has been an awakening through Consciousness within them to come to aid and inspire Earth and its' inhabitants. It is helping to cause a revolution as an awakening of positive energy is invading much of humankind as our hearts reach out for answers. Above all, it is the action of Love that motivates. Many have come but more are expected.

During our lifetime, we will see many changes occur. You will experience many changes within yourself.

Truth is being revealed. Much knowledge is being given. Transformations are occurring. Not all will accept what is transpiring. Their beliefs will keep many stuck in their old ways. Throughout the Cosmos they are coming to help nurture those that are questioning worldly reality and strengthen those who already embrace Enlightenment. Fear will continue to take hold of many but fear cannot exist where there is Truth and Divine Love reigns. Though Love will be felt not all will perceive and allow themselves to see the many lifeforms that exist. Some will think them to be imaginary.

The entire world will be challenged to expand its' previously limited way of thinking due to what is now becoming known, seen, and photographed. There will always be an opportunity to either accept or deny what you see and experience. The opportunity to ascend to another level is yours. Our cosmic family is here to help.

The photo reveals many different life forms. Within this particular photograph the Rings are transporters. They can come and go. As you open your heart to the awakening, open it also to the many Lifeforms that exist in our dimension and others. They are here to help us. They cannot do otherwise as Love, and concern for this Earth, is creating this wonderful opportunity.

Chapter 20

Earth-Cradle Of Life

For many centuries, the Western world and Middle East have believed that humanity has existed for 6,000 years upon the Earth. Only over the past 50 years have archaeologists given the 'educated world' permission to expand that time-frame. Archaeology along with religion has controlled much of what the world has come to believe.

As in Religion, archaeology has had its renegades. There have been some unafraid to propose other possibilities, pushing the envelope. Most of it based on actual discoveries. This type of archaeologist has received much ridicule within the profession. They tend to be 'black listed.' Many more archaeologists remain silent on the issue even though they know there is evidence that blows established beliefs out of the water. As in religion, the world of archaeology has looked truth in the face and declared it unfit for analysis and scrutiny. Heresy!

The world of discovery is entering into all aspects of our lives and into all cultures, with the flow of information over the web, disrupting the normal flow of belief. We are being bombarded with theories and possibilities on all fronts. Archaeology and religion are being forced to rethink their positions on creation and evolution. More discoveries are being made regularly. The professional world is being forced to reevaluate the way things have been done in the past. The commercial world we have created isn't working. Religion isn't working. Theories presented in the past that were declared heretical and completely insane are now being reviewed and even accepted in some cases.

Worlds In Collision

Emanuel Velikofsky, a renowned scientist in the 1940s' and 50s', was completely ostracized from the scientific world upon publishing 'Worlds in Collision.' Controversial, to say the least. Among other theories, he believed that the planet Venus was, at one time, on a different orbit than it is now, possibly even a comet. It approached Earth close enough to cause worldwide catastrophes, tying the event in with Biblical records. In its near collision with Earth its path changed and it eventually found its present orbit.

Velikofsky went on to theorize that if the surface temperature of Venus could be measured it would be several hundred degrees because it was still cooling down from its previous life and orbit.

When Voyager entered the atmosphere of Venus more than twenty years later, Velikofsky was vindicated when it sent back temperature readings of the planet at more than seven hundred degrees, yet nothing was ever said in the media about the Velikovski theories.

The world of science had to rethink everything it had presumed true up until that time.

Mars

The same is occurring with the planet Mars. All the exploration, from the 1970s' until today has shown evidence of intelligent life but the scientific world hides it and even claims it does not exist.

When evidence of an entire city, or the remnants of one, were photographed in Hale Crater, the scientific world wouldn't even acknowledge it was there when it could be seen by anyone who chose to look. Not only Hale Crater but dozens of other sites all over the planet had, at one time, been built up, industrialized, and farmed. Evidence of underground operations can also be seen, yet the scientific world insists on sending more probes to see if there has ever been life on the red planet. They have to have it their way. The attempt to continue brainwashing and the proliferation of misinformation continues to this day.

As we access Universal Consciousness all assumptions and theories are put aside. As I have stated before, all answers are within. The knowledge of the Universe is encoded in our DNA. We are all connected. We are all One. We are all part of Supreme Creator.

As we are able to access our Higher Self, we tap into Prime Creator. We move closer to fulfilling the purpose of our physical creation.

At this point in our evolution we are learning more about these vehicles that we inhabit. They are a marvelous creation. Through them we experience emotion at an accelerated rate, otherwise it would take millions of years, if ever, to reach the same level of Love and Compassion that we will have learned through incarnations.

Earth

Earth was designed and created just for that purpose. It has been the 'cradle of life' for this entire solar system. There have been many civilizations planted here, flourished for tens of thousands of years, then left the planet by one means or another. Some civilizations were destroyed through natural catastrophes, some were caused by power hungry leaders along with creator gods, similar to what is happening at this time, while a few cultures or tribes did ascend to higher dimensions. Not all civilizations upon this Earth were Homo-Sapiens, yet every created lifeform that has inhabited the Earth has been a vehicle for Consciousness.

At least one culture left Earth to seed other planets including Mars. There has been some speculation that life from Mars seeded life on Earth, but it happened the other way around. Earth has been the cradle of life for this solar system. Creator gods have assisted at times but only if it was of benefit to them.

It is very arrogant for us to believe that we are the only species of human to have enough intelligence to propose going to another planet to perpetuate our species, and that we can do it with the present technology. When we left Earth to populate Mars, other planets and moons, our technology was much more advanced than what we have today and evidence will be, and probably already has been, unearthed. We are lead to believe that we have not even advanced past the internal combustion engine that propels our cars. The fact that we still need cars is a sign that we are still in the dark ages, still being deceived and lied to. Technology for more advanced propulsion has been known to certain factions of the military and some governments, especially the US. It has been controlled and hidden from public knowledge for economic and strategic purposes as well as for power and greed.

Some awakened individuals in previous civilizations knew how to move objects of incredible weight and size simply by using sound, vibrations. They did not require the wheel. They knew how to 'tune in' to the Universal Grid and manipulate harmonics in a safe way, to move objects, even themselves, through space and time without disrupting the flow of life and nature.

That knowledge is still available but will not be demonstrated or publicly allowed in our present state. There are those powers still in office that would see it misused. Those that do know how to use it will only do so in secret. Likewise there are those that can move from one vibration to another because their Consciousness is awakened to that level. It is not 'rocket science.' It is simply opening up to 'Consciousness', awakening to our true identity. When enough of us have done so, the world, as it is at this time, will not be able to exercise powers that it has at present. Governments will diminish, religions will no longer have the power they have exercised over the past millennia. Borders will of necessity soften, or in some cases disappear and we will truly be moving toward one family, not a one world government.

Some Cycle Of Civilization Statistics

Geologists tell us that the Earth is 4.6 billion years old. If we allow the first four billion years to prepare the Earth for life, it leaves us with 600,000,000 years of 'cycles of civilization' to have been here during that time. If we use 100,000 years as a 'cycle of civilization,' there would be 6,000 cycles during that time alone.

Archaeological forensics has only found skeletal evidence of our present civilization going back 13,500 years. Some megalithic sites are now being dated back 17,000 years. If we give the archaeological world an additional 9,000 years, equaling 26,000 years per 'cycle of civilization,' we come up with 23,000 cycles during the last 600,000,000 years.

The chronology of humankind upon the Earth is available to those who seek it. Very soon, as the Antarctic ice sheet breaks up, archaeologists will be confronted with a real dilemma. They will be finding remnants of very advanced civilizations, not necessarily Homo-sapiens, that have been hidden from us by creator gods along with governments in the past to further control the flow of information regarding the true history of Earth and humankind during our cycle of civilization. They will have to acknowledge our interstellar connection with innumerable species of life, and that we have never been alone. That some of us are more advanced than those creator gods because of our desire to use Love and Compassion and reject the limits that they, along with mankind, insist on due to their lack of ability and desire to expand their Consciousness. This movement to Enlightenment is death to religion and governments.

Keepers Of Mother Earth

Earth has been dealt a short hand through this present cycle of civilization. There have been small cells or groups of indigenous tribes that, to this day, still honor Earth. They are 'Keepers of Mother Earth.' They know we are not alone in our journey and that we shall not ascend without

Her. Mother Earth is in the Ascension process at this very moment. She is moving through the necessary stages just as those individuals who want to ascend. There will be some catastrophic events taking place. Events much more dire than we have experienced to date, but this is all necessary as Earth ascends.

These are times of great fear for those that do not, or will not understand. Earth must go through these changes. As it does there will be a separating of the new world from the old. Those of humankind who are choosing to ascend will move on with the new Earth. Those still believing religion is their salvation will remain and witness the continued violence and destruction that is presently infecting the Earth, while the new Earth and its inhabitants continue the process of Ascension even beyond the perfected physical form to that of 'Light Beings', moving out into the Universe assisting other worlds in their Ascension process. All this because of Love and Compassion for Creation and Life exercising free-will.

The Thirteenth Hour

The history of time has been completed. Now is the time of the 'Thirteenth Hour,' the hour of mystery, the hour of the unknown to the unawakened. All of history is at our disposal. All can be recalled, reviewed, made right, revealing the dark intent of our so called historians.

The power of the pen is now exposed and the frequency containing all of Earth history is available to those who know how to access it. It reveals the intent of certain creator gods and those of humanity in coercion with them. The knowledge of the creator gods has been passed down to certain mortals from generation to generation, in secret. Creator gods are intradimensional beings and hidden in frequency, now being exposed.

Hidden artifacts of Earths' true history are about to be revealed. Along with these artifacts are tools and teachings of techniques used in engineering to produce huge stones and structures. Objects of such great mass that with todays technology can be reproduced but not transported by todays earth moving vehicles. Techniques which todays engineers cannot comprehend but soon will be able to experiment with and find more lost secrets of past engineering. This will completely change the direction of design and engineering presently used. Also the storage of information in stones and crystals is now being revealed and will assist us in the Awakening.

A Column Of Cosmic Light

Visualize yourself in an ascended state. As you meditate, bring a column of light from the cosmos through your energy centers and into Mother Earth. Now, while maintaining this column of cosmic light, visualize another column of light rising from the Earth and traveling back up the column that descends. You are completing the cycle, a Cosmic Circuit.

As in my photographs, during rainstorms, as visible light is ascending back into the heavens from the Earth, you are creating and maintaining your own connection between Heaven and Earth, Earth and Heaven. Listen, sense, enjoy the presence of Prime Creator. You are Prime Creator. Prime Creator experiences all of your journey through this process. From your birth on Earth in the third dimension through your process of Ascension that continues on through infinity. Incorporate your own internal light with that from Earth and the Cosmos.

Chapter 21

Healing & The Healer

We as mankind have been so conditioned and brainwashed over the millennia that we don't think we have the capacity to do things ourselves, that we have to depend on inspired political and religious leaders for our guidance and direction. Without these vicarious leaders, puppets of the intradimensional gods, we are lost and defeated from the start.

Prior to organized religion itself, Oracles, throughout history, have assisted these false prophets and leaders, all in the same vein, to wield power over those that can be deceived and manipulated, many times even deceiving those very leaders themselves. These Oracles and Psychics implanted the teachings of a savior to be born of a virgin, crucified, and rising from the dead, more than two millennia prior to the advent of the Jesus story which eventually lead to the organizing of the 'Universal Church.'

The world has been conditioned to ask that very church, and other 'spin-offs' of that church, for answers and direction. The same psychic energy used before the Universal Church then slithered its way into the organization.

Even the the religion of my ancestry, not a break-off of any religion, has been infiltrated. In their calling and ordination, Patriarchs use their psychic abilities, incorporated with specific statements commanded by the Priesthood, to give an 'inspired' message regarding the future of the individual receiving the 'Patriarchal Blessing.' All linked back to a life of service, obligation, and sacrifice within the Church, the Mormon reality.

At the age of thirteen I received my own 'Blessing.' I memorized it and kept it in my heart, believing my good actions and deeds would help to make the message come true. It stated that I would become a husband and father to 'sons and daughters'. That never happened while in the church. I became a father to four daughters and a son. The addition of another daughter and son came in 2006 when Dery and I were married. Though they are not my biological son and daughter, they are, along with my own children what I refer to as 'hijos de mi corazon,' children of my heart! The fulfillment of that portion of the Patriarchal Blessing took place far away from any Church.

Another prediction given by the Patriarch, declared I would stand before great congregations and stretch forth the 'truths of the Gospel.' It is true I have at times stood before great congregations, and many small ones. Some of the congregations were within the religion but many more outside of it. I can say with assurance that what I say to groups and congregations is not the truth of the gospel of that religion. I encourage all people to go within to seek truth. Go where you are required to go and experience what is necessary to find and embrace it. I found much of my incentive for truth while within religion. Mormonizm was one of the greatest stepping stones to assist me in this extraordinary adventure while teaching me how to overcome the fear in delivering messages to any size audience.

As I reflect on many of these experiences I've had, I am moved upon much more by the message and blessings my father showered upon me in the family garden when I was a boy.

My experience with psychic energy over the years has been quite revealing. This includes how I have received and interpreted messages from other lifeforms in other frequencies and dimensions, also how I have observed it in others people claiming to be gifted psychics. The giving of a message to another individual, who believes they do not have the gift themselves, is a tremendous responsibility to be honest and honorable in the delivering of that, assumed to be, divine message.

Many psychics, when not completely tuned in to the vibration of the individual, and not protecting their own vibration, can give a misleading message. The message can interlace information received from the psychics own experiences, many times negative, with the person seeking counsel from higher Consciousness, and wanting to know how to proceed with a particular situation or relationship.

This can be even more crucial when delivering a message the psychic has received regarding the seekers health.

What About Healing?

I have received messages from many different psychics over the years, many of them unsolicited, many of them accurate, others not so accurate. Some attempting to 'tap into my energy' without my permission. Having the connection with my higher self allows me to tap into my own energy in seeking information about the health of my vehicle/body. If a psychic tells me I need to see a doctor I immediately question the message and the psychic. I have become acutely aware of my physical status. I also know that even though I am involved in the Ascension process my body has been perfectly created to follow through with the programming it received at its creation, that includes and involves illnesses that I am to experience in this lifetime. If the message is confirmed through my 'higher self' I will have it checked out. If not then I am instantly aware that I was misinformed. I question this person. I also reject the message. A true psychic taps into that energy field, it is true, however, that person can be deceived into believing that all messages from that frequency are always correct. THEY ARE NOT! Those of that frequency are fallible and many times no more accurate than the opinions of those we rub shoulders with every day. I have witnessed many people claiming to be gifted psychics when all they are doing is playing the individual and expounding the power of suggestion. This can be done on an individual or mass basis. History has proven this to be true. What it comes down to is that these charlatan psychics are promoting their own form of religion. You have a right to access your 'higher self' about your own physical status.

Ignorance is a Choice

Someone I've known for many years recently contacted me to ask for prayers regarding the discovery of possibly fatal growths in various organs of his body. I was a bit surprised he contacted me since he is still active in the Mormon religion and is aware of my history within the church but has chosen to find out very little about me other than what his Mormon friends have told him since my leaving that reality. I sensed his fear in the request not knowing what the results of the tests would be.

When I am asked for prayer concerning illness or other personal challenging situations in an individuals life, I take it very seriously. Before responding to the request I went within my heart to seek guidance on how to proceed. I then formulated my response and answered thanking him for asking for my prayers and assured him I would follow through with his request. I also included exerpts from 'Healing & The Healer'.

A week passed before hearing from him again. I was thanked for my prayers and told that he didn't have time to read the words I included in my response. He would read them sometime in the future when he felt like it.

He is very well read in the medical field having worked around it for several decades. He has also fought off other cancers and cystic growths as well as benign tumors in the past. He chooses to listen to what medical books and opinions have to say rather than going within to find self-guidance and healing. We are what we think. We can be nothing else. If we choose not to listen to our heart and ignore the cry of the physical vehicles need for assistance from the Cosmos, our Creator, then we continue on in ignorance, by choice. Perhaps he will grasp it in another lifetime while he continues to suffer through this mortality, again, by choice.

Where Do I Go For Answers?

Quoting from <u>Path of Empowerment</u>:

'The widespread breakdown of the physical body, which has become a worldwide health crisis, makes a profound statement about the lack of pleasure and quality of life that is experienced by the dwellers of the so-called civilized world. The surfacing of deep emotional and physical pain among the people of Earth is a collective expression of a constriction of consciousness, which is based on foundational beliefs about what is and what is not possible. Humanity has developed a collective unconscious fear of having to take care of itself, and this belief creates a direct blockage of power in the body. Physically, the blockage, or obstruction, of energy can manifest in a wide variety of patterns that create chaos within the body's internal systems. The belief in a supreme being who will save you, or eventually judge and punish you for your transgressions, only serves to further discount and deny the magnitude of your power to heal your life from within.

Beliefs that focus on pain are plentiful in your world, and they appear to be justifiable because of experiences that appear to be real; however the intense focus on the expectation of pain and suffering is actually what brings them about. Beliefs in pain have been woven into your biology; they hold court in your subconscious mind, often making you wary of life. Unresolved issues such as bitterness, anger, or wounds and death traumas are carried over from other lifetimes, often appearing as mysterious pains and chronic aches in the body. The patterns in your genes hold memories of previous lives as well as the story of your genetic bloodline'.(page 146)

Observe what is happening all around you. You are your best psychic. Believe you have the power, ability, and gift to lead yourself to good health and Awakening. Encourage others to do the same. Where do you go for answers? Go within! Observe how you physically and emotionally respond to your intent to heal your body and your mind. You will notice some subtle and not so subtle changes. Enjoy better health through your intent, through understanding Consciousness and how it learns from your physical vehicle and how you can teach your body to be more sensitive to your higher energy, to the Cosmos and your interdimensional family.

You may be required to seek out medical assistance. The key is to allow your Consciousness to inform you of the need, when it does, act! Don't do it simply because that is what the world expects and demands of you. Once your connection to Higher Consciousness is reestablished, the way is very clear and there may be times when your journey requires the help of the medical establishment. The most important part of your journey is reconnecting with your Higher Self. The need for medical assistance ceases to be guesswork since you know what is required of you through your intuitive self.

Chapter 22

Comments & Journal Entries

Upon beginning my international employment, over the next twenty years, I would experience many different cultures and beliefs most of them through international contracts.

Having lived in eight different countries and worked and taught in more than thirty countries, I realized early along the way that I was as much the student as I was the teacher. I sought my classroom out in the world but was following my own passion, not someone else's. I did realize the responsibility of following the directives of the organizations I worked for, after all they provided the door of opportunity to introduce me to the many countries and cultures, all due to my background. I came to realize that an international banking background would never have allowed me to know the many cultures at such an intimate level.

I observed along the way that those who wanted to know the truth, but were unwilling to pay a price for it, listened to the teachings and preachings of others. Seemingly well-intentioned, faithful, indoctrinated preachers and teachers with diplomas in hand from Seminaries and other schools of 'higher learning.'

With these official documents and certificates they earned the right to be called Reverend, Pastor, Bishop, etc. These ecclesiastical graduates are generally elevated to a high standing in the community while given the overused title of 'man of God.' The benefit of a doubt given to them, with the church members paying for the privilege with their tithes and offerings giving lay-members the clear conscience desired and the justification of continuing to promulgate the overall generally accepted way of Christian life.

I can't help but feel their twinge of guilt while offering up their structured prayers. Guilt in the lack of dedication to seek out and passionately follow the pathway of truth rather than the pathway of culture and religion. They are so engrained in the world culture of money and materialism that they teach their children with the same passion they should be demonstrating in the seeking of Higher Self and Consciousness. They couldn't find within themselves the strength to step out on their own. Their Love of money and material possessions is much more than their Love of self and following the Spirit desires of their own Heart. They will eventually find their way. If not through an awakening while in this life, then it will happen in another.

The amazing event happening on Mother Earth right now is noticed by many worldwide. Many people are opening their hearts to this Universal, Interdimensional offering of Love by those Entities and Lifeforms that have arrived to assist all with a desire to change this world to a more accepting sphere of Unconditional Love. The Love with which Creator brought Earth into existence.

<u>Journal Entry</u>
8/4/2014

Earth is known throughout the Universe as a sacred creation. One that shows forth Infinite and Unconditional Love. Great numbers of individuals and groups of lifeforms have come here and will continue to come here from all over the Universe to experience it, to touch it, to 'set foot' on it, to commune with Earth. She is a perfect creation.

In Meditation

At 1:00am I witnessed an unusual cloud in the sky. I knew it was concealing a craft. I focused on the underbelly of the cloud, a few hundred feet above me. As I did a form began to come into view. The bottom of an OVL became visible as the cloud began to lift and the craft descend at the same time. The form was that of a rectangle, approximately 50 feet long and 25 feet wide. It continued to descend until it stopped about 2 feet off the ground, the cloud disappearing, leaving the craft completely visible, right in front of me. It was approximately 12 feet high.

There was an inset in the side of the craft about 4 feet wide and 3 feet in, revealing access to the interior of the OVL. The vehicle was opaque. I could see into the interior and even natural light filtering through from the other side. I stepped into the inset, turned to my right and extended my hand to touch the base framework of the craft. My hand descended through it. As it did I felt a strong field of energy. The entire OVL was made of this organized energy.

I noticed a movement and turned my head to the left as I saw a female form descending a staircase inside the vehicle then exiting through a doorway immediately to my left within the very inset where I was standing.

I saw two people moving around on the second level inside the vehicle where the female occupant descended from. As she exited the OVL we began to talk to each other. Children from the immediate area came up to both of us as we all began to interact with each other. The scene closed.

The Perception of Reality

We create our own reality through thought and intent. Whenever we think about something that is to take place and imagine how it will unfold, we create the future. We interject our intention for the result based on what we perceived in our thought process.

As we move forward, experiencing the once future event, we move our actions to mimic our intent. If we cannot exactly mimic our intent we adjust our actions to accomplish our goal. We then have, once again, changed the future.

The End Of The World

Creator gods have played with mankind from the beginning of this cycle of civilization. Throughout time they have revealed specific events and dates when this world would end. They have even planted in peoples' minds, visions of how it would occur. The more important thing they instilled isn't the event, but with devious intent they planted and nourished fear in the hearts and minds of the believers of something that was prophesied by them to take place, yet never has.

People, then, alter the coming 'end of the world' by making excuses for these creator gods and further feed them through their fear while anticipating the event and their own destruction or resurrection. Fear is food to these charlatans and there are millions, even more, ready to follow them and put their lives on the line daily to prove them right, as they continue to allow themselves to be manipulated and deceived while continuing to worship them.

Message from Thought

The way of Source is through Love. Love is Creation. Love is the Creator. Love is also Light and all that Light encompasses. The act of creation is done with joy through vibration and sound, all encompassed in Light.

Source gifts us with that very same ability. In our human form creating life was meant to always be done through the sexual act inseparably connected with Love. This sexual act of Love begets offspring that cannot be duplicated in a test tube nor through artificial insemination. The artificial act of impregnation denies the passion involved in a true act of sexual bond. In human form we have learned to create outside the natural act of Love.

The Cosmos are not meant to confound us. There are those in human form that attempt to continue to control humanity by insisting that religion is good and was introduced by God providing the only way to return to Him. The thinking of these individuals is linked directly to the creator gods of history. They introduce teachings attributed to ancient sages who have guided them on trips of intellectual fantasy. Explaining the ins-and-outs of creation and the numerous levels of powers and priesthoods that those who are enlightened can embrace to ascend. The prerequisites needed to continue in the Ascension process. Their explanations are so sophisticated and complex that one can get lost in studying the process as written down for these students of Ascension to purchase and begin to follow the same as any other organized religion that has been manipulating and controlling mankind from the beginning of this cycle of civilization. These comments include the writings of those claiming to have had contact with Enoch, Jesus, Moses, Elijah and many more that claim to know the secrets behind creation and salvation and sin and repentance. WHERE TRUTH EXISTS THERE ARE NO SECRETS! If someone is promoting a specific way to return to God, they are confusing creator gods with Source. They are promoting themselves and other creator gods.

The Illuminati, New Illuminati and other so called New Age religions that seem to spring up in all directions are attempting to promote their own agendas. No different from main stream religion.

What is happening at this time in our history is the revealing of truth and the exposing of lies. That is why we are seeing so much corruption being brought to the surface. Corruption in government officials and organizations, in religions, in the banking system worldwide. We are witnessing genocide at every turn, violation of human rights and the right to live in freedom. Even in the western world individual rights are being trampled on and ignored. The governments are manipulating the system in a way that its citizens are being herded into a paddock of fear, fear of losing their home, their ability to earn an income, terrorism, constant human blood sacrifice with the use of legal or illegal firearms. All in the attempt to give up total control to the power hungry. They want many to abdicate their power of thinking. Rampant manipulation of the system and the western world's love affair with materialism separates one from Nature and connection to Earth.

This is what appears to be happening in the world today. But, as the Masters have shown us, what appears to be happening is not true reality. What the world wants us to believe is not what we are involved in. We control our own frequency, vibration. It is this frequency modulation that allows us to enter other worlds, other realms of existence. To embrace, again, the Love of Source that created us and gifted us with that same power of creation, through Love.

The Hollow Bone

Hollow Bone teachings have been with us for thousands of years. Our ancestors knew of them and practiced them passing them down to following generations. These teachings never fail. One learns to listen not only with the ears but more so with the heart.

The idea is to become like a hollow bone, a conduit, accessing the Universal Consciousness where we have no fears. Where only Love exists and egos and pride disappear. We become teachable, all wisdom available as we move into a higher vibration of Consciousness, one with Supreme Creator. Spirit can come directly into and through us.

When a person has such a great desire to rise above their own culture it is due to the longing to know more than the present world is willing to divulge. To rise above the culture can mean walking away from tribal conditioning, religious or political conditioning and even family conditioning, or all of the above. When one does follow this desire they open a door to the Universe. They can access the knowledge that has always been there.

Ground yourself to Earth and the Universe. Be one with it. Let your energy flow into it and allow its energy to flow into you. Listen with your heart. Become as the 'Hollow Bone.'

Hollow Bone Photography

What a wonderful feeling ran through me as that first picture appeared on my computer screen. A voice inside told me had told me to take a picture of the sun while in the Colombian countryside with my wife. I couldn't make out too much detail on the little 2 1/2" screen of the digital camera, but, I could see some small colored dots around the sun itself. I would have to wait a week until we returned home to Florida.

At home in Punta Gorda I stared at the computer screen for some time then picked up my camera and went out into the back yard.

It was a clear morning. Florida had been experiencing a drought for some time so clear skies were not unusual. The air was crisper than when I took my first photograph in Colombia the previous week. I turned the camera on and pointed it toward the sun. Again as I took the picture I could see some activity on the camera screen, much more than the first photo.

I walked quickly into the office in the house and uploaded it into my computer with a twenty-three inch screen.

How beautiful the menagerie of colors and designs but nothing had prepared me for what I was about to experience as I put it into the edit command and zoomed into the beautiful detail. There on my computer were brilliant colored orbs. Some large but most of them smaller. All the different colors of the rainbow. The scene reminded me of an intense light shining through a prism. But these were not divisions of color as a rainbow, all the colors were throughout the orbs. The largest orb was just above and to the right of the sun and about half its diameter and the surface of the orb was dimpled like a golf ball. As I surveyed the other orbs in the picture I saw faces peering back at me. There was no mistake. The two distinct faces I saw looking back were faces I had seen in my meditation a week and a half earlier. There was no camera involved in my meditations. I was so amazed and delighted to now be looking at them on the computer screen.

There was no doubt in my mind nor in my heart that what I was feeling was spiritual, and I was allowed to photograph it. My immediate thoughts were of sharing this wonderful occasion with my wife and also the entire world. Here was visible proof of a higher dimension. My love for Source and the Universe took on a greater meaning. My peripheral vision had expanded spiritually. I had always believed in, and expected higher knowledge was directing me in my life. Now my physical eyes were looking right at it as my spiritual vision increased exponentially.

I took more pictures the next day. There were some differences in the positioning of the orbs but others remained where they were the day before. Some days there were more, some days less. But they appeared in every photograph. Cloudy days were sparse but when the clouds did appear the light from the sun and orbs were dispersed and very little orb activity could be photographed.

About three weeks into my new adventure I heard the voice again. "Take pictures of the night." I did, and from the first nights photo's all of my pictures contain orbs. Some more concentrated than others. Some contained "sprites" near the ground that would show up in different solid colors; white, blue, yellow, green and red.

I continued taking pictures both day and night and created albums to keep track if them. I began taking pictures of the moon in its various phases and studied its movements across the heavens. A magnificent creation. The earth would not exist in its present form or location if it were not for the moons' present position. How did it get there?

One night while photographing the moon I noticed a strange cross shaped object of different colors that at first I thought may be the space station. I got on line, looked at photos of the space station and quickly determined they were not related. What was it then?

As I continued, other odd objects would appear in my photos.

I took a photo one evening looking toward a 60 foot pine tree in our back yard. I observed the large orb on the cameras screen but couldn't make out any more detail than that. As I downloaded it to the computer and zoomed in I could see the outline of what I thought was an Indian chief that appeared to come up out of the orb with headdress on, in full costume, standing erect with his arms stretched down and back, his chest out, looking or worshiping towards the half moon. As I meditated on it the next day I was instructed that it was a 'shaman'.

I kept up my routine and for a period of time, every five days or nights, I would be visited and shown other 'life forms.' At times I wondered if they were vehicles sent to observe me. I came to realize that they did come to observe and interact with me but they are not vehicles by our description (three dimensional), they are organic, alive, and are here to communicate and deliver messages.

The fifth dimension is opening up into our present world. It can be, and is accessed by those who are prepared. These messengers are not harbingers of doom, to the contrary, they are bringers of Light. They are ambassadors of Love sent to all humankind. As I take more photographs of the orbs and life forms more is being revealed to me. This world is changing and people are seeking like never before. The answers are available for those who seek. For those who know what it means to become a "Hollow Bone." I, myself, am the conduit!

The Hollow Bone

Supreme Creator never asked to be worshiped, just to Love and be Loved.

God did not create hell, religion did!
God did not create religion, man did!
The gods of history are not thousands of
years more advanced than us. They are
only a 'thought process' more advanced
than us, and they are not gods!

To worship gives one the opinion that there is something higher than love. There is nothing greater than love nor higher. Worship is a term and a commandment taught to humankind by religion. Source only teaches and radiates love. Worship is left to lower life forms who cannot grasp the truth about Source, those who refuse to open their eyes to access Consciousness. Creator just wants to be loved.

Higher learning is accessed through "Universal Consciousness", knowledge without end. This is the true classroom setting for learning.

I'm giving you a glimpse into the heart of God. Supreme Creator is not complicated. Supreme

Creator does not issue commandments, does not demand to be worshipped.

Earth has a soul (Consciousness). Although Source gives everyone free agency it was intended that humankind would become one with the Earth. Mankind invented a way through creator gods for everyone to "pay as you go," introducing greed and power so certain individuals, as well as those so called gods, could rule others.

Supreme Creators way is that all humankind be blessed by the Earth freely, and give back to the Earth freely.

The Earth is moving into a higher level of Consciousness and is recompensing man for its misuse.

As the Earth moves into a higher level, those of humankind who are aware of this can also move into it. They are connected to the Earth, Universal Consciousness, and to Source.

Evil-An Invention of Religion

Evil is an invention of religion, as is hell. Evil does not create. Evil only destroys. God is Supreme Creator. Love Creates. Love is Creation.

Humankind exists throughout the Universes. Humankind has the ability to create on a subordinate level. Humankind has used ego with some of its creations to confuse and control. Creations through Source are only done through love. Love is the power to create at the highest level.

Creation at lower vibrations can and has been realized on this earth like none other. Thus Supreme Creator has intervened after millennia of purposeful confusion created by beings that only want to control through cults, religion, governments, corporations, etc. The world has been given sufficient time to correct its perverted direction.

The many, including the earth itself, who have been persecuted by powers such as these, have cried out for deliverance. Creator has heard and is responding. Those who appear to be the greatest and most powerful on this earth will be ensnared in devises of their own making. Bound by their own greed and appetite for power.

Government and military secrets
will soon be revealed.
Capitalism will eventually crumble.
Borders will eventually disappear.
We will truly be one family.
Where in capitalism does it encourage
us to 'love our neighbor'?
Religion is being exposed and
will crumble with much pain,
anguish and discomfort.
Humankind will live without fear.
Death will be exposed as a lie.

Authors Comments

As we look at the world today we can see much heartache, much destruction, and a direction by many in the East towards eliminating anything that stands in the way of a one world religion. At one time in the past the Universal Church tried the same thing, directing their inspired hatred, in the name of their god upon, not only Islam and judaism, but shortly thereafter the entire western hemisphere.

It has never been completely successful on either side but has been the cause of hundreds of millions of deaths in the names of these perverted gods, leaders, and religions.

Finally the moment has come in the history of this Earth when there will soon be a separation. The Earth and this solar system has entered into a new cycle. The exposing of Consciousness is infiltrating the existing physical reality. The reality we have been conditioned to believe in is fading into history and being replaced with truth, Divine Truth that has always existed but been masked over by those intent on control by deception.

We are perfect creations, perfect multidimensional creations. These dimensions, where we exist, are revealing themselves. Where we thought we were alone, we now find we are not, and never have been. Not only do we find other lifeforms, we find other extensions of ourselves. We are understanding that our DNA is much more than we could fathom in just a three dimensional reality. We find that what we were told was real, is not, not even close!

Understanding that we inhabit these physical bodies, or vehicles, to gain experience in and through emotion is paramount and signals the very beginning of our awakening. Upon receiving this revelation we have unlocked the door to Higher Consciousness that allows the flow of Light and Energy to resume as it once did.

The Awakening is an individual event but cannot be fulfilled without involving those around us. An individual is not an Entity of Consciousness if it is not connected or linked to Supreme Creator. It simply cannot exist.

Then the statement should read, 'Wherever Consciousness can exist, Consciousness does exist!' 'Wherever Light can exist, Light does exist!'

We Are All Children

Children of Mother Earth, turn inward. Listen to the stillness within. Do not listen to the mind, invite the heart to reveal itself to you. This is the doorway to Higher Consciousness. What you will now experience is the vibration of the Cosmos, of Infinity. You can now listen, hear, and see with your Consciousness the way you were meant to at your Creation.

Love Mother Earth as she shows forth her Love to you. Show forth Love to all children of the Earth. No child is less deserving than another. All are creations and extensions of Supreme Creator. We are all Children of Source. Love yourself and all of humankind. As you do this you begin to change the world. This is not accomplished through the mind, it is done through the Heart, one person at a time.

As you seek more and more Divine Knowledge you awaken to Creation as you were meant to. Understanding of the Cosmos increases. In this metamorphosis you notice the absence of fear. You see yourself in the Divine Light of Source.

While you realize you are still in a physical body, you are even more aware than before of your place in this world. You move forward within the same body as before, yet there is a great difference in how you see all that is around you and view the reality you have created with new vision. Your sense of duty to the Earth has taken on the new reality of your Creation as you move forward aware of your connection to Source. You are in the same vehicle but your mind and the worlds conditioning is no longer the driver, Consciousness is.

About the Author

Life's Inspiring Journey

Life is a journey and like every journey there is a destination. The destination prescribed by our parents is mostly based on their desires for our success and happiness based on their life experiences.

As we walk our way through life we are met by obstacles and challenges. Some of them placed there because of our own doing. Some placed there due to following the path that was chosen by our parents and we feel obligated to follow so as not to disappoint them. More obstacles are placed there because of other outside influences that have convinced us that they know better about what is needed in our lives than we do.

These are the same experiences that the author has dealt with in his life. With one single comment his father made to him at age eight, his life journey would take him to many far away places in search of truth. Truth he assumed he would find in the religious and social teachings of his parents. Four generations of ancestry couldn't be mistaken. They were all seeking the same thing he was. He had to find the truth where his father told him he would, but he didn't.

With a profound desire to not only find his direction in this life but also to help inspire others to do the same, he has found great happiness and peace in sharing his life experiences with all people. Having lived in eight different countries as a professional in his field he has witnessed much turmoil socially, culturally, religiously and economically in every country he has lived and worked.

His powerful story and witness has reached the hearts of many throughout the world. This journey of the soul is his journey. His connection with that Higher Source is felt in his words and in his desire to help elevate the Consciousness of all humankind. To increase the vibrational level of the Earth that he loves so dearly.

The destination he has sought in his life is within view. His experiences and incredible library of Energy & Light photography are having an impact on lives across the globe. His message can help change your life.

Moshe

Printed in the United States
By Bookmasters